HOW TO GET
TO THE
FUTURE
BEFORE IT
GETS TO
YOU

Also by Shepherd Mead

Shepherd Mead

HOW TO GET TO THE FUTURE BEFORE IT GETS TO YOU

HAWTHORN BOOKS, INC.
PUBLISHERS / *New York*

Contents

4

WOULD YOU TRADE YOUR AUNT LUCY FOR THE BATWINGED HERON?

Or, Do you realize that for a sizable segment of the population, ecology is just something for the birds?

5

"HOW MANY PEOPLE DO WE NEED?" "HOW MANY CAN WE STAND?"

Or, How to use "population" against people

6

CATCH-23

Or, The Third World and what you can do with it

7

HOW TO USE PEOPLE-POWER

Or, How to become a spare-time scourge of public and private environment-busters

Contents

8

SEVENTY-SIX TROMBONES AND
FIFTY THOUSAND Ph.D.'S   81
Are the corporations doing anything
to save the earth?

9

YOU AND ME AND THE GNP   99
Or, Our gross national product and
what we can all do with it

10

COMMUNICATIONS: THE
UNTOUCHABLE WONDERS   106
Or, How to keep people from a future
that's already in the past

11

THE ELECTRICAL PARADISE   118
How to make your home
the center of the world

12

13

14

15

16

Preface

THE END OF THE WORLD
AND HOW TO ENJOY IT

Would you like to tell the future to go away? Are you fed to the teeth with doomsday men? Weary of cashbox Cassandras? Unshocked but troubled by future shocks? Nerves jangled by computers that say we're doomed if we do and doomed if we don't?

Have you heard all the latest ultimate predictions? Have you read Dr. Paul Ehrlich's statement that "the battle to feed all humanity is over—hundreds of millions are going to starve to death in spite of any crash program embarked on now"? Have you seen William and Paul Paddock's *Famine Nineteen Seventy-Five!* which reckons we'll just have to write off whole countries and let them starve to death? Have you heard that all economic growth must be stopped today, or there will be almost unimaginable catastrophes?

Now we have a kind of doomsday one-upmanship.

The fellow who predicts that the world will end (horribly!) in 2020 is one up on the lad who said 2030, and if you really want to hit the best-seller list and have the top lecture dates, it's better to say 2010, and tell everyone those other chaps were optimists.

Do you believe all that? Is it really hopeless? Are you trying to decide whether to crawl under the bed, or just jump into the river?

Well, hold it a bit. Wait till tomorrow. I felt that way, too, about a year ago, and decided to wander around in the future and see what it's like. And I can tell you now, quickly, in case you're standing on the windowsill about to jump, that you can sit down again. There are still one or two things we can do.

Don't tell all of "them" I said so—but things could even get *better*!

HOW TO GET
TO THE
FUTURE
BEFORE IT
GETS TO
YOU

1

DOOMED IF YOU DO AND
DOOMED IF YOU DON'T

Or, How to get the world
out of a black box

What started me into never-never land was the vast
and noisy circus of the Club of Rome, striding across
the Sunday supplements, banging its drums. Here was
a group of European industrialists who had organized
a study, financed by the Volkswagen Foundation and
carried out by a team of experts at Massachusetts Institute of Technology, with enough graphs and figures to
fill a whole book.

And it said, loud and clear, that the whole world
faced catastrophe within about fifty years and that this
wretched present we're now suffering through may
well be the Golden Age, a kind of heavenly pinnacle
from which we shall almost certainly stagger down-
ward into the infernal abyss. And almost any forward
motion, certainly any economic growth, will only make

things worse. Practically any step we can take will be disastrous.

Surely, I thought, any statement made under such auspices—I mean, M.I.T., and all!—must be true. I got the graph-loaded book, *World Dynamics*, written by Jay Forrester and the computers of M.I.T., and studied it. I had never felt so shattered. It seemed to me that any effort was useless.

Each of the computer graphs was a kind of mathematical scenario of doomsday. Now, I've usually written a kind of satirical-philosophical science fiction about every ten years, to say all the things that seemed to be unspeakable in any other tone of voice. So I decided to try to dramatize, in a science fiction exercise, one of the computer *Götterdämmerungen*.

First, let's examine the way these computer predictions work. There's nothing supernatural about using facts to foretell parts of the future. You find out how much of everything you have and how fast you're using it up. If you have two pounds of coffee and use a quarter pound a day, you can accurately foretell your coffee future: in eight days you'll be out of coffee.

Systems dynamics people call the amount (the two pounds) the level and the rate at which it is used (or refilled) the flow. What makes it complicated is that all the factors influence all the others. If the normal coffee-drinking population at your house is raised from four to six, your rate of coffee flow will increase. And the coffee-drinking population might be reduced if the coffee-drinkers knew you were running out of coffee—

so the coffee level might influence your breakfast-population level (i.e., some of them might decide to get their coffee on the way to work). The principle of systems dynamics is as simple as that, but when all the factors of world levels and flows are combined, it become mind-boggling, and only a computer can make all the millions of continuous calculations.

In planning his computer "model" of the earth, Jay Forrester decided to set up five basic levels: population, natural resources, capital, the percentage of capital used for agriculture, and pollution. All these five levels keep changing, and the changes in each "feed back" to the others, either increasing or decreasing them. For instance, more population requires more food and hence more agricultural capital (like plows and tractors), and this reduces natural resources (metals, diesel oil for the tractors, and so on), and also raises pollution levels. (See Graph 1.)

If the earth were unlimited in size and resources, the curves could move ever upward: more people, more farm machinery, more food, more capital to control pollution, and so on. But the earth is a small planet floating in space, with limited land and atmosphere and resources and places to put our rubbish. So the curves turn down, and often the one that's dropping like a rock is—*us*!

Almost any short-term remedy, anything that could work over a period of twenty years or so, may be the worst thing we can do for the long run, say, fifty to a hundred years from now. Just reducing the birthrate

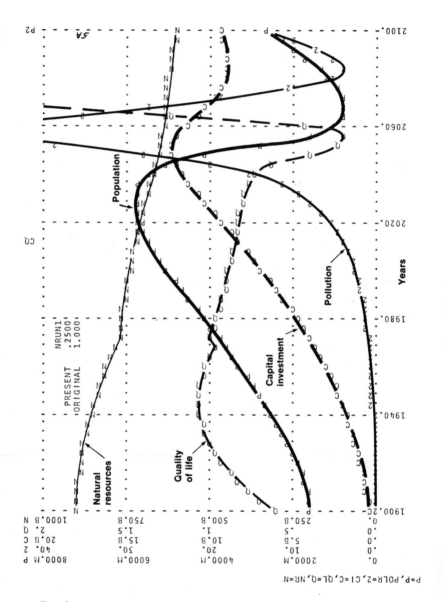

Graph 1.

Reprinted with permission from *World Dynamics* by
Jay W. Forrester. Copyright © Wright-Allen Press, 1971.

can still lead to a pollution crisis.[1] Cutting down on pollution still allows population and capital investment increases to cause disaster.[2] It has, in fact, already happened.

Forrester says, "Many of the problems the world faces today are the eventual result of short-term measures taken last century."

If all that sounds forbiddingly mathematical and graph-icle, let's try to translate a computer conversation into normal English. For example, a typical off-hand remark of Jay Forrester's to his computer would go something like this (in fact, it is taken right out of the book):

Forrester (*earnestly, on keyboard*): BRMM. K=TABHL (BRMMT,MSL—)

You might well say, "How's that again?" But the computer knows he's talking about the birthrate material multiplier and the "K" time stop, and please do look up and interpolate the table of birthrate material multiplier, material standard of living, and—well—and so on. It's the way a computer and its closest friends talk to each other, and there's no poetry in it.

Let's take Jay Forrester's graph interrelating the five basic levels and talk to the computer about it, keeping all the actual figures but putting it into plain language. (See Graph 2.) Computers, you know, always talk in capital letters:

"Are you there?"

"YES, SIR. AT YOUR SERVICE."

"Now, you did this graph, didn't you?"

7

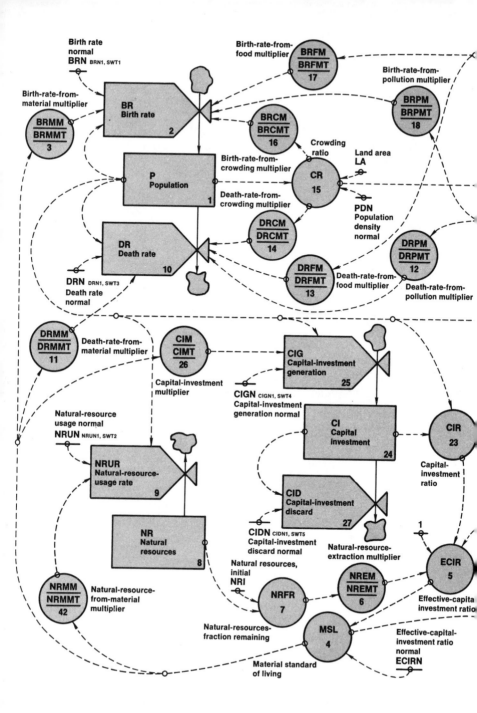

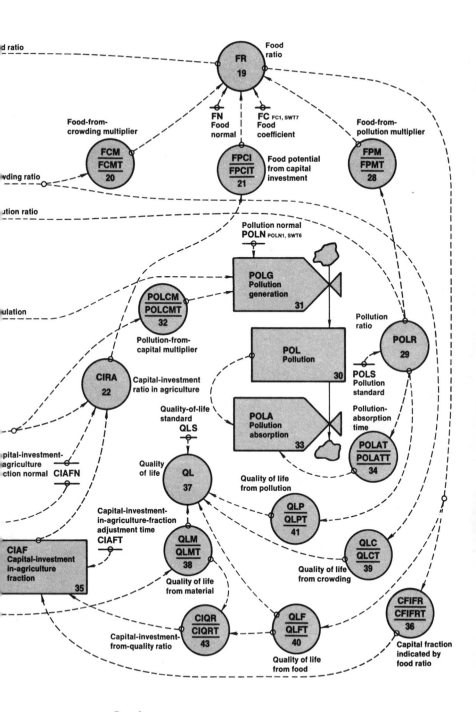

Graph 2.

Reprinted with permission from *World Dynamics* by
Jay W. Forrester. Copyright © Wright-Allen Press, 1971.

"WELL, I DID THE ARITHMETIC. MR. FORRESTER PUT IN THE DATA, SIR."

"Now, that top curve, the one going steadily down—"

"YOU MEAN THE NRUN 1, SIR?"

"Beg pardon?"

"SORRY, SIR. I MEANT THE NATURAL RESOURCES USAGE NORMAL."

"Does it always run downhill like that?"

"OH, YES, SIR. CAN'T GET ANY MORE NATURAL RE-SOURCES, CAN YOU, SIR? AND THIS TIME WE JUST ASSUME THAT THE POLNI IS—"

"Come again?"

"SORRY, SIR, THE NORMAL POLLUTION LEVEL—WE AS-SUME IT'S LESS THAN NORMAL TO START WITH IN THIS PROJECTION, SEVENTY PERCENT OF NORMAL. WHAT WE'VE DONE IN THIS ONE IS TO SEE WHAT WOULD HAPPEN IF WE RAISE THE CIGNI—THAT'S CAPITAL INVESTMENT GENERA-TION NORMAL—RAISE IT JUST TWENTY PERCENT."

"Right, we spend twenty percent more on capital investment, and I can see that everything's going along fine. By 1985 the population is up a bit."

"UP ABOUT A BILLION AND A HALF, SIR."

"People are happier?"

"I DON'T HAVE THAT, SIR. THERE'S JUST THAT MIDDLE CURVE, QUALITY OF LIFE."

"Down a bit."

"BIT MORE CROWDING AND POLLUTION, SIR, BIT HARDER TO BREATHE, AND NATURAL SWIMMING ALMOST FINISHED.

BUT WITH THE EXTRA TRACTORS AND ALL, THEY'VE GOT PLENTY TO EAT."

"Let's jump ahead to about 2025. Schoolchildren of today would be in their sixties."

"ACTUALLY IT STARTS ABOUT THEN, SIR."

"What starts?"

"POPULATION COLLAPSE. SEE THAT CURVE, SIR?"

"The one going almost straight down?"

"YES, SIR. THE POPULATION HAS REACHED SEVEN AND A HALF BILLION, AND BY 2044 IT IS REDUCED TO ONE AND A HALF BILLION."

"Reduced by six *billion* people? Why, why?"

"DURING THAT TIME, SIR, THE POLLUTION REACHES FORTY TIMES WHAT IT IS NOW. BIT OF A PROBLEM BREATHING. EVEN WORSE FOR THE CROPS."

"You're saying that people—our *children* and *grand-children*—are suffocating and starving?"

"YES, SIR. RATE OF ABOUT A MILLION AND A HALF A DAY BEYOND NORMAL DEATH RATES."

"A million and a half bodies every day—for *years*?"

"FOR ABOUT TWELVE YEARS, SIR. IT'S ONLY AN AVERAGE. SOME DAYS MORE, SOME LESS."

"A million and a half a day, little kids, pretty girls—"

"I CAN WORK OUT AN ACTUARIAL BREAKDOWN ON IT, SIR—"

"And all we did was increase capital expenditure twenty percent?"

"YOU WANTED A BODY BREAKDOWN, SIR? NUMBERS OF MALES, FEMALES, UNDER TWELVES, AND—"

"Cry when you say that!"

"CRY, SIR? I HAVE THE LACHRYMAL GLAND FIGURES, SIR. WITH AIR POLLUTION AT THAT LEVEL, TEAR PRODUCTION SHOULD WORK OUT TO ABOUT TEN TIMES NORMAL. IN MILLIGRAMS PER EYE, SIR, IT—"

"Stop it!"

"BEG PARDON, SIR. DID YOU WANT THE TEAR LEVEL BEFORE THE—"

"Never mind! What happens after that?"

"REGULAR HEAVEN ON EARTH, SIR! POPULATION DROPS, POLLUTION DOWN. JUST LOOK AT THAT QUALITY OF LIFE CURVE, SIR. RIGHT THROUGH THE CEILING!"

"Where will that lead?"

"POPULATION WILL RISE AGAIN, SIR."

"And it all happens all over again?"

"I CAN CONTINUE THE PROJECTION AS FAR AS YOU LIKE, SIR. WE'LL HAVE TO START WITH THE NATURAL RESOURCES LEVEL DOWN THERE, WHERE WE LEFT IT. ONLY A NEGATIVE FEEDBACK ON THAT, SIR—"

"It's worse next time?"

"THE QUALITY OF LIFE, SIR? BOUND TO BE LOWER, IN EACH CYCLE. LOWER AND LOWER EVERY TIME, SIR."

Now those figures are all accurate, in accordance with the M.I.T. computer. Does it frighten you? It scared the very daylights out of me, a calm prediction that about a million and a half extra people—beyond the regular death rate—would starve or suffocate or die horribly in other ways *every* day for about twelve years, and in the very near future, affecting people who are alive now.

I tried to do a science fiction dramatization of this, how people would act and talk during such a period. I found that my characters would be forced into scenes like this:

"Darling, it says on the stereophonic, 3-D holographic, smell-oriented TV that there are now thirty-five million people in New York, and a hundred thousand are dying in the street every day. True?"

"No problem, pet. The bulldozers push them into the East River. Going to work wonders for our quality of life. Anything new while I was at the office?"

"Not really, darling. Another eight or nine people tried to cut through the barbed wire around the garden. Starving, you know."

"Shot them, of course?"

"Yes, dear. Threw them on the compost. What's new with you?"

You have to *assume* an attitude like this if you accept the fact (as the M.I.T. computer and Forrester do) that nobody is doing anything about all this.

Could there be something wrong with this dynamic system? What if we investigated the system itself, in its own way, talking to the computer? Now, the figures used to make the graphs are based on what computer people call exponential growth, meaning anything that grows at a fixed percentage every year, causing the total to double and redouble every so many years. Suppose we could talk with our same M.I.T. computer about it:

"Could you help me, please?"

"HAPPY TO, SIR."

"I'm making a study of historical pollution in New York City, beginning in 1850. Are you writing this down?"

"OH, YES, SIR. POLNY 1850. GOT IT."

"The problem was chewing tobacco and horses."

"YES, SIR. CHTO AND HO."

"And the main problem was spit and horse manure."

"YES, SIR. CHTOSP AND HOMAN."

"I'd like to set up a dynamics system on this."

"NO PROBLEM, SIR. JUST GIVE ME THE LEVELS AND THE FEEDBACK LOOPS, AND WE'RE OFF."

"The spit level in the gutter was half an inch, and the manure level in the middle of the road averaged half an inch, too."

"YES, SIR. CHTOSP LEVEL .5 IN., HOMAN LEVEL .5 IN. DO YOU HAVE THE FEEDBACK LEVELS, SIR?"

"They were feeding the horses oats and the men plug cut tobacco. By 1860 the rates on both of these doubled."

"SUPERB, SIR. IT'S JUST LIKE WITH MR. FORRESTER. YOU'VE GOT AN EXPONENTIAL SITUATION THERE, SIR."

"You know how to deal with that?"

"OH, YES, SIR. POSITIVE FEEDBACK LOOPS AND LEVELS RISING EXPONENTIALLY. YOU'VE GOT A LEVEL THAT DOUBLES IN TEN YEARS."

"Can you project that dynamically?"

"WON'T TAKE A NANOSECOND, SIR. WE'VE GOT A CHTOSP LEVEL OF 1.0 INCH IN 1860, 2.0 INCHES IN 1870, 4.0 INCHES IN 1880."

"Just give me the readout for 1970."

"YES, SIR. [*Short buzz lasting 1½ nanoseconds*] I MAKE IT THAT BY 1970 WE HAVE 2,048 INCHES OF SPIT IN THE GUTTERS AND 2,048 INCHES OF HORSE MANURE IN THE STREETS. THAT COMES TO 170 FEET 8 INCHES OF EACH, PRECISELY. WILL THAT BE ALL, SIR?"

"Yes, thanks very much."

"ANYTIME, SIR. WE'RE HERE TO HELP YOU."

So by systems dynamics, using these exponential figures, it can be proved that life is utterly impossible in New York City—a fact that some now feel to be true, but not because the population is buried under a pile of horse manure some fourteen stories high and drowned in nearly thirty fathoms of brown spit.

We should of course remind everyone that this is a model, and like Mr. Forrester's models, it doesn't take into consideration the fact that people are paying attention. In other words, we might expect that when the spit level and the manure level reached the second or third story, people would begin to do something about it.

Of course, you have to be careful about short-term measures. For instance, birth control for horses might have helped. We have a situation like that in a chart in *World Dynamics* (page 102) where the birthrate (for people) was reduced, but after twenty years (presumably just out of sheer cussedness) it goes back up again, even though it is by this time fairly obvious it will lead to utter disaster. Or, with available oats, the horse population would rise to meet it, in accordance with the Malthusian law.

One thing about computers is that they haven't any *sense*, unless you put it in. That computer would have gone on figuring exponential horse manure until the year 3847, at which time the manure might fill the whole solar system—unless you happened to tell the computer that the horse would phase out for something else, even the bicycle.

The serious scientists began jumping all over *World Dynamics* and its companion volume, *The Limits to Growth*, by Dennis L. Meadows (a systems analyst) and his wife, Donella, based primarily on the computer figures. The first objections, in quiet, studious magazines like the American *Science* and the British *Nature*, were that the Club of Rome shouldn't have made quite so much of a circus out of it, hiring publicity men, calling press conferences, and whooping it up like the launch of a new wowser by Jacqueline Susann.

The founder of the Club of Rome has an answer to that. He is Aurelio Peccei, a former executive of Fiat and Olivetti, long concerned about the predicament of mankind. He had even written a book about it himself, called *The Chasm Ahead*. He and his club members had traveled all over the world for two years, trying to

get political leaders to listen: "Our message was re-
ceived with sympathy and understanding, but no action followed. What we needed was a stronger tool of
communication to move men on the planet out of their
ingrained habits." He felt that the M.I.T. study and
the books permitted "every layman to enter the laby-
rinth of the fantastic problems towering over mankind."[3]

There's no question that the problems are stagger-
ing.

The first of two main scientific objections is that the
world model is based toward collapse "by assuming
that new technologies and resources grow at linear rates
while everything else grows exponentially."[4] Or, that
the horse manure goes up, decade by decade, like 2, 4,
8, 16, 32, and so on, whereas the technology of street
sweeping only goes up like 1, 2, 3, 4, 5, and you can't
keep up with horses that way. And it isn't true. Technology is increasing very rapidly, as we'll see.

The second main scientific objection was illustrated
rather dramatically by a team working on a computer
in Amsterdam.[5] They said, in effect, "He left out the
social feedback," or, as I said above, the fact that somebody might do something about it. This book is social
feedback. If you decide to compost your garden waste
instead of burning it, that's social feedback, too. The
Amsterdam group set up its own dynamic system, put
in a social feedback loop, and that gave the future "a
much more stable outlook."

In fact, paradoxically, Forrester's graphs and book themselves are really social feedback, if they don't terrify people into freezing, like a rabbit, and doing nothing, thinking that nothing can be done. The whole aim of the Club of Rome is deliberate social feedback.

The point is not that it is evil to make computer models of the planet. Forrester says, and I agree, that just "thinking about" world problems isn't enough by itself, because the factors involved are too complex. A computer can help, and this was just the first, trial attempt. The only mistake was in blowing it up as the final answer to everything. We mustn't stop making dynamic models of the earth; we must make much more sophisticated ones.

In fact, the worst thing that could happen is that concerned and conscientious people like Peccei, Meadows, and Forrester might be ridiculed into stopping, and I don't think they will be. Peccei certainly hasn't stopped, nor has the Club of Rome as a whole. Dennis Gabor, a member, and a Nobel Prize winner in physics, is now making a technical study on problems of energy and recycling. Economics professors Mesarovic of the United States and Pestel of West Germany are working on a survival model, and so on.[6]

We *are* in a dangerous position, but it is nothing like as hopeless as you might think by reading *World Dynamics* or *The Limits to Growth* or by listening to some of the really irresponsible doomsday predictions. True, if we don't start doing something now, the situation could grow desperate within our own lifetimes, or those of our children.

But there are very many things, as we'll see, that can be done, and that should be done quickly.

2

ANOTHER MAN'S POISON

*Or, "Do I really have to go in two
directions at once to save the earth?"*

If you want to join the war to save the planet, the main
battleground is the ecology and environment front.
And if you're eager, as I was, to wade in right away, you
might ask, "Exactly what's the problem, and what do I
do now?"

And the simple answer to that is "Well, they haven't
quite made up their minds."

So, our first mission is to try to help them make up
their minds, or at least to make up our own. "Them"
are the countless squabbling, angry, righteous, debunk-
ing, greedy, saintly—well, *every* kind of—ecologists,
environmentalists, biologists, chemists, propagandists,
and all the rest.

Ten years ago not one person in a hundred even
knew what the word "ecology" meant. The Oxford dic-
tionary says it means a "branch of biology dealing with

living organisms' habits, modes of life, and relations to their surroundings." It comes from the Greek word for "house," because it describes the housekeeping arrangements of living things. Today politicians are saying, "Ecology is like motherhood," the one thing it's always safe to be *for*. Or, as one of the Earth Day people chalked on a New York street, "If you're not part of the solution, you're part of the problem."

And one thing is certain: There's going to be a lot of talk about ecology on the way to the future. Many believe it's the ultimate key to survival. And some feel it has been so overdone it's becoming ridiculous. As one professional ecologist told a congressional committee in 1970: "Ecology is no longer a scientific discipline—it's an attitude of mind."[1]

The Four Ages of Ecology

1. *The Primitive, or Little People, Stage.* This stage was by far the longest, lasting millions of years, from the first man to the beginning of the industrial revolution.

Ecologists all look back wistfully to this gentle-people era, before we had the clout to knock nature around. We were part of the ecology of the planet, instead of the opposing force. We were just swept along with it, and whenever we weren't able to cope, that branch, that tribe, that race was simply ground under the gentle heel of Mother Nature and became extinct, starved, frozen, or eaten. And since we hadn't been supplied with claws, fangs, shells, or even fur to keep us warm, or almost anything else physical, except a thumb, which enabled us to hold a club, we had to live entirely on our wits.

Were we ecologically angelic? Whenever we were, it was just that we didn't know any better. We certainly had no inborn sense of conservation. As far as we could tell, the earth was endless; you could always move on someplace else. We thought nothing of burning down a forest to drive out the game, and evidently one of our earliest agricultural tricks was to set fire to the whole area and let everything burn down. It was much easier than chopping down all those trees with a stone ax. Then we hacked up the ground and planted seeds. This often resulted in runaway erosion and the ruining of the land. When nothing would grow on it but grass, we put our goats on that; they ate it right down to the ground, and then there was desert. So what? With only a few million people in the world there was always plenty of land. We moved on, ecologically amoral, so few of us that the planet could repair most of our damage.

2. *The Mechanical Age.* This has lasted less than two centuries, during which time we've managed to do more harm than we had in the previous several million years. We arrived at the Bulldozer Age, when our idea of ecology was to knock everything down and then dump chemical fertilizers, weed killers, and pesticides over what was left. Another decade or so of this, and

there might not have been anything left but the insects.

3. *The Doomsday, or Here-We-Go-Tippy-Toe-with-Mother-Nature, Age.* This was a natural reaction to the Bulldozer Age. We'd gone so far that somebody had to scare us to death. The most dramatic, and one of the earliest, screams of warning came from Rachel Carson's *Silent Spring*, which erupted out of *The New Yorker* to become a best-selling book in 1962.[2]

Rachel Carson had the unfair advantage of being a trained biologist and also a skillful writer and propagandist. She showed that the new chlorinated hydrocarbon insecticides, like DDT, killed not only the insect pests but their bird and insect enemies, too, often making the situation worse than it had been before. And the poisons were almost indestructible, building up in the bodies of birds, fish, and humans—all the way to the penguins in the Antarctic.

Silent Spring's many true case histories of destroyed wildlife frightened everyone and resulted in severe restrictions on the use of hydrocarbon insecticides in the United States and many other countries. And it created an almost hysterical rage against everything chemical, and often against everything technological.

Should we really just return, tippy-toe, to Mother Nature, let the insects eat each other, and occasionally our crops, or us? Are all the works of man evil? Are all chemists villains; is all technology vile?

This whole area is now a violent battleground, and before we get any closer to the future, we'll have to sort it all out.

We now hear reputable scientists scoffing about "the silent spring mentality." We have the statement of the man who may well have saved more humans from starvation than anyone in history, Norman Borlaug, Nobel Prize agriculturist, and father of the "green revolution," developer of many of the new grains that have, among other things, stopped famine in the Far East, at least for the time being. Borlaug refers to the "silent spring arguments" against all chemicals (especially fertilizers) as "vicious, hysterical propaganda."

John Maddox, editor of *Nature* magazine and one of Britain's most illustrious scientific journalists, has written an almost warlike book, *The Doomsday Syndrome*, trying to shout down all the prophets of doom, including overemotional ecologists in general, and scoffing at many of the statements of Rachel Carson.

We have left-wing activists suggesting that all the furore about wildlife and wilderness is almost fascist propaganda, that conservation is really rampant conservatism—and just look at Hitler! There was a real wildlife lover! You can find quotes from Adolf about the clean mountain beauties of Berchtesgaden that sound almost like the Sierra Club. In fact, the whole "Sierra Club mentality," say the activists, is just a ploy to take our minds off capitalist oppression, to preserve lovely, pristine playgrounds for the rich.

How are we going to get to the future this way? Are all the great ecologists wrong? Should we just crawl into our holes and wait for the end?

Let's step back quietly and listen to the best known

of all the ecologists, Barry Commoner, author of *Science and Survival* and *The Closing Circle*. In the latter, newer book he gives us some good specific case histories. The first, called "Los Angeles Air," is a documentation of automobile pollution, beginning with the early 1953 Ford Motor Company pronouncement: "The Ford engineering staff, although mindful that automobile engines produce exhaust gases, feels these vapors are dissipated in the atmosphere quickly and do not present an air pollution problem." (Ford, as we'll see later, has come a long way since then.)

Dr. Commoner takes us through the whole battle, the partial reduction of the waste hydrocarbons and the increase of the nitrogen oxides and the photochemical smog. Very few people would quarrel with these facts. But Dr. Commoner makes statements at the end of this chapter: "Air pollution is not merely a nuisance and a threat to health. It is a reminder that our most celebrated technological achievements—the automobile, the jet plane, the power plant, industry in general, and indeed the modern city itself—are, in the environment, failures."[3] The new moderates, like John Maddox, object to blanket statements like this. They would say (and I would agree) that technology itself is not bad, only that the relatively primitive technology of today is faulty—actually, that it's not technological *enough*. Our first step was a stumble, but more sophisticated technology can put us right.

Barry Commoner's corn-belt case history, "Illinois Earth," is another good one. He shows how Illinois farmers, by using too much nitrogen fertilizer, have poisoned the water supply, especially that of the city of Decatur. The nitrates, converted biologically to nitrites, can asphyxiate and kill babies.

The farmers, certainly not deliberate villains, found it difficult to grow corn economically without ever-increasing doses of nitrogen fertilizers, and of the excessive amounts, some is not absorbed by the corn and drains into the water supply. Dr. Commoner's scientific teams have been working with the farmers to try to solve the problem, and what they learn may help with similar situations in California, Israel, Germany, and probably anyplace where nitrogen fertilizers are used excessively.

It's in the battle of Lake Erie that we can see best the difference between the evangelical, crusading ecologist like Barry Commoner, and the antidoomsday people like John Maddox. Dr. Commoner gives a seventeen-page analysis of the problem in his chapter called "Lake Erie Water," the sad and true story of the metamorphosis of a beautiful lake into a biological tragedy —the destruction of the sturgeon, the end of the mayflies, the reduction of oxygen content, the algal "blooms" that turn the water into a kind of pea soup, and eventually a lake that is almost an open sewer. However you look at it, the result is frightful. Dr. Commoner concludes: "We have grossly, irreversibly changed the biological character of the lake and have greatly reduced, now and for the foreseeable future, its value to man."[4] True, almost certainly, but it could give us the idea that there isn't much point in doing anything.

John Maddox, on the other hand, doesn't dispute the Commoner biological facts, but tells us that all isn't completely lost. ". . . Throughout the 1960's, the lake somehow managed to support a thriving fishing industry. In 1970 it yielded 25,000 tons of fish. . . . The proclamation that the lake is already dead . . . has if anything given Lake Erie more prominence than it deserves."[5] Perhaps we'll do better if we realize all is not lost.

The doomsday criers make us feel that everything is getting progressively worse. And so it is, in some places. Should we give up? Not at all, says Maddox. Wherever men have really rolled up their sleeves and got into it, they've made extraordinary progress and have often reversed the trend.

Take the River Thames as an example. Once it was really a sewer. "In the 1870's it was customary for the House of Commons to be protected from the stench from the river by hanging wet sackcloth over the river terrace." This I know is no longer the case. "In recent years," writes Maddox, "the condition of the river has been measured by the distance over which it is almost devoid of oxygen in the late summer. By means of stricter controls of effluents discharged into the Thames, the distance has shrunk dramatically from more than twenty miles to much less than ten miles."[6] And more recent newspaper reports say that fish are returning to the river near London.

To quote Maddox again: "The quality of water in San Francisco Bay has so improved in the past twenty years that the shrimp are returning, and the fishing has been improved."[7] This was no accident; it was caused by a great deal of sewage treatment.

The old "pea soup" London fogs, which I remember, and which were caused largely by the burning of soft coal in fireplaces, have completely disappeared. This was no miracle of nature, just the result of the very strict rules of the Clean Air Act of 1956, making smokeless fuel compulsory. It resulted in a 50 percent increase in winter sunshine in London.[8] Anyone who has lived in St. Louis or Pittsburgh knows how much the air in both these cities has improved. No apocalyptic forces of doom were involved in any of these conditions; they were all caused by the foolishness of men and were all remedied by the intelligence and energy of men.

John Maddox goes after Rachel Carson's *Silent Spring*, too. It "introduced and made respectable the most vivid form of the now common literary trick by means of which readers are given an awesome account of what might happen and are then advised that the full horror of this prospect can be avoided only if people and public institutions act more responsibly."

Maddox knows it is not good to dump DDT over everything, but it is not the "elixir of death" that Miss Carson pretended. In fact, he says, "DDT is no more poisonous to people than aspirin," a statement that startled me as much as it may startle you. We once used things like lead arsenate on insects, and we fumigated with hydrogen cyanide, both of them *really* poisonous to people. Maddox is irritated most of all by Miss Carson's suggestion that insecticides like DDT are likely to cause cancer in humans. There is no proof of this at all, and he felt it was "irresponsible of her to have so chilled her readers with hints of horrors which are so badly founded as this."[9]

A very levelheaded pair of ecological observers are Barbara Ward and René Dubos, and their book, *Only One Earth*, is one of the best I've seen. It is subtitled *The Care and Maintenance of a Small Planet*, and one reason it is so good is that it was commissioned as an unofficial report by the Secretary-General of the United Nations Conference on the Human Environment. A draft of it was sent to consultants from fifty-eight countries, many of them from the Third World. Their comments were incorporated into the book and give it a truly planetwide point of view.

It is easy for us, sitting in a cool climate with insect screens on our windows, to have righteous indignation about DDT. It is quite another thing if you live in the tropics, where malaria and sleeping sickness attack almost everyone. One of their United Nations consultants informed Ward and Dubos that "he probably would be dead if DDT had not been available at the time he was working in Guyana," and "many others repeatedly assert that millions of people will soon die of infectious disease or malnutrition if attempts are made to limit drastically the use of pesticides in public health practice and in agriculture."[10]

As Ward and Dubos say, "In parts of Asia up to a quarter of the harvest may go to feed not humans but predators. Corn output may increase by 60 percent, potatoes by 70 percent if their resident pests are eliminated."[11] Statistics to us? In these countries it can mean thousands of starving children.

On the other hand, some of their consultants "are convinced that natural ecosystems are even now profoundly disturbed by pesticides and . . . predict that the Earth will progressively become unsuitable to human life if present trends of pesticide use are continued."

You can see it isn't a simple problem. It depends on who you are.

Make the Easy Smokestack Test

If you're thrown into a mixed ecological group, here is one way to sort the people out! Find any good picture of an unidentified high smokestack, belching black smoke. If you don't have a picture, lean out of your window, any window, and take one. All you need to do to make the people-sorting smokestack test is to show it around. You will get various comments:

1. *The doomsday comment*: "What did I tell you! We can prove by computer that this smokestack, and 67,894 like it, all belching smoke like that, increasing annually and exponentially, by 1990—see that curve?

—will suffocate 89.8 percent of the population, or 13 billion, 500 million people!" (And of course he may be right, if nobody does anything about it.)

2. *The technological activist*: "Great! Just the thing for our new automatic fly-ash precipitator! If we could sell one to each of the 17,822 factories using them, our GNP would be up 1.8 percent!" (And it might be, at that.)

3. *The delegate from the developing country*: "Beautiful! We are building one like that now in Boppu-Aboola! Even higher! Enough kilowatts for lights and tele-veesion for every house in Boppu!"

"Will it smoke like that, too?"

"Even better! Like great feathers of black ostrich! You will see! Look out modern world! Here comes Boppu-Aboola!"

You may think the Boppu-Aboola attitude is bad, but did you spend your youth walking in back of a musk ox? And you do have electricity now, don't you—most of the time?

The shouting match between the evangelists and the debunkers is sure to go on and on, and a great many books will be sold in the process. But the best antidote for shouting is a specific example. What are some of the things that have already been done successfully?

Some Specific Steps

The best answer to the insecticide argument that I've found is a case history from the Ward-Dubos book.[12] It happened in the Cañeta Valley in Peru where DDT and other chlorinated hydrocarbons were used to spray the cotton crop: "The sprays killed the pests. They also killed the killers of the pests. By the time the original pests had developed DDT resistance, all their old 'beneficent' enemies had vanished. The pests multiplied, even more applications had even less effect and before long the whole crop was in jeopardy." The silent-springers would say, "Aha! We told you so!" But wait. There's more.

"However, the Cañeta Valley case history has a happy and significant ending. Overall spraying with all-purpose insecticides was abandoned. Beneficent predators were introduced from outside, planting and harvesting were timed to avoid the times of infestation, highly specific insecticides were added to the total 'system' and, as a result, the cotton crop recovered. A single-shot effort was abandoned in favor of a mix of natural, artificial, and also traditional methods." Yet Ward and Dubos add: "No effective alternative [to DDT] has been found for dealing with the problem of malaria." There aren't easy answers for everything. Maybe not for anything.

As for pollution, one suggestion that has been made by many is to put it on a pay-as-you-pollute basis. An ingenious book was written almost entirely around this idea, and oddly titled *TANSTAAFL*, an acronym for "there ain't no such thing as a free lunch."[13] The author, Edwin G. Dolan, a Dartmouth economist, thinks the trouble is that pollution has always been free. The factory just dumps the waste into the river, and that's that—no charge.

Let them do it, says Dolan, but just put a stiff price on it, so many dollars per ton of pollutants. You might even, he suggests (with tongue slightly in cheek), put up all the nation's rivers and lakes for auction and let the highest bidder buy them and regulate their use in a businesslike manner. "If General Motors owned the Mississippi River, it would surely charge for the privilege of dumping in it, and would presumably also consider bids for conservation groups and communities to keep parts of it clean for bathing and fishing." And if they didn't, I might add, they'd have Nader after them again! In any case, if people had to pay the full economic cost of pollution, they'd soon find a way to stop it, and meanwhile the "pollution tax" would go toward cleaning up the environment.

Does this sound like a wild dream? It isn't. A system like this has already been tried in Germany, and it's working beautifully. There was a pollution problem in the Emscher Valley of the Ruhr. The main difficulty was that about two hundred different municipalities were involved. So they set up an overall authority (comparable to our Tennessee Valley Authority or the Port of New York Authority) and accepted the principle that those who produced the pollution must pay for cleaning it up.

In this case the charge was based on the amount that the pollution reduced the oxygen content of the rivers, as measured by the BOD (biochemical oxygen demand) figures. The effluents were checked and tested, and charged in proportion to BOD damage. The charges enabled the valley authority to build treatment plants, dams, aeration and land drainage facilities, storage lakes and waterworks. The authority makes a profit on the water, though its prices are the lowest in Germany, and spends the equivalent of $60 million a year.[14]

The price paid by plants for pollution encourages them to invent new ways to reduce it. Many of them have not only reduced these costs, but have actually made money on metals and minerals recovered for recycling. Sulfuric acid, for instance, can be recovered from the pickling liquor in steel manufacturing, canning industries can recover salable vinegar, and paper industries, shifting from sulfite to a sulfate process, have reused their chemicals and cut their pollution as much as 90 percent.

Not only that, say Ward and Dubos, thermal pollution can be put to good use, too.[15] Hot water (say, from nuclear plants) can be used (as the Japanese and Russians are now doing) to make warmer fish-farming ponds and fatter fish. Some American power companies are experimenting with warmer-water oyster beds and quicker-growing oysters. Warm-water irrigation can make plants germinate more rapidly, and pumping warmth into the lower depths of Lake Erie and Lake Ontario might bring pollution to the surface and help to remove it.

One of the most important things, Ward and Dubos

say, is to create a single responsible authority. They cite the case of the Ohio River: West Virginia, on one bank, has fixed 86° F. as its top temperature, whereas, on the other bank, Ohio says it can go to 93°! As long as we have such silly conflicts of authority, our hands will be tied.

We've hardly begun finding out the ingenious things we can do with waste. Chicago piled up refuse and made a ski hill out of it. Name? Mount Trashmore! As it grew higher, the skiing got better. India, of course, has been burning cow dung for years; it's the main fuel for cooking. St. Louis is now shredding refuse, mixing it with pulverized coal, and burning it in power plants. A ton of trash equals half a ton of coal.[16]

Barry Commoner suggests there is no need to dump sewage into rivers. Pipelines from cities could send treated sewage to agricultural areas, where it could replace at least some of the chemical fertilizers.[17] For years it has been normal procedure in England to remove organic materials from sewage, return clean water to the rivers, and sell the treated organic material as fertilizer.

The big Bull Run Steam Plant near Oak Ridge burns five tons of pulverized coal every *minute*—and produces almost no smoke or air pollution at all. Precipitators trap 950 tons of fly ash every day. It's used for landfill—an improvement over our traditional method of scattering it over the people! Anyone could do it— there are many companies that make this kind of equipment. It just costs a little more.[18]

All these things are part of "social feedback," and they can knock the stuffing out of the M.I.T. doomsday graphs. In fact, the estimates are that it would cost us about 1.5 percent of our gross national product to eliminate virtually all pollution. We *can* afford to eat the banana and pick up the peel. Don't we want to do it?

That's three ages of ecology—and I think the fourth age needs a chapter of its own.

3

THE FOURTH AGE OF ECOLOGY

Or, "Natural" isn't necessarily good

The Fourth Age of Ecology is just beginning to dawn. I once thought I'd invented it. I called it creative ecology or, if you will, man-made or artificial ecology. Eventually this will have to come if we're going to get all the way to the future.

It began to happen the first time somebody stopped talking about Mother Nature in a hushed voice. There is not now, and there never has been, anything necessarily maternal, or lovable, or even beneficent about Mother Nature. On a spring day on a flower-bedecked meadow beside a gurgling brook, she does seem gentle and poetic—a kind of barefoot madonna.

However, it should be mentioned to the skipping-along-with-Mother-Nature ecologist that nature is also poison ivy and stinging nettles, mosquitoes, termites, woodworm, and the tsetse fly, scorpions, rattlesnakes, and sharks, tornadoes, earthquakes, floods and tidal waves, rotting teeth, tapeworms, cancer, Mongoloid babies, syphilis, and the black plague. Behind her sometime look of the lovely barefoot madonna, she can be an idiot bitch, mindless beyond cruelty. Not even knowing you're there, she'd as gladly starve you, freeze you, burn you alive, or give you the screaming meemies, as waft the scent of her honeysuckle to your natural nostrils. (The honeysuckle doesn't give a rap for your nostrils; it wants to be cross-pollinated.)

Nature has no love and no law but survival. Nature —in fact, the whole planet (and even, as far as we know, the entire universe)—is a floating crap game, and nobody, up to now, has ever been shown to be intelligently in charge. Perhaps now is the time.

If there is any guiding biological force, then its method must be "Let the dice roll." Let 'em die. Only by dying by the trillions, even by the millions, of *species* has life evolved. Only by profligate, ever-present death has there been, or can there be, life. It's all written plainly in the rocks, in a billion years of fossils, death beyond imagining, beyond counting, leading to new life, to *us*. To us, so far. We're certainly not (or at least not necessarily) the end result, nor do we have any guarantee that we won't just join the other fossils, while new species carry on. Nature wouldn't shed a single tear. She has no tears to shed.

There has never been a shred of evidence that any beneficence has ever existed biologically, nor, for that matter, any malevolence either. Nor is there any proof, as Jacques Monod keeps saying, that there is any *purpose* in any of it—nor, I might add, any proof that there is *no* purpose—nor is there any reason why we can't make one of our own.

The miserable survivors drag themselves up on the beach one more time to prepare for the next battle, which will never be the last. Survival is all, at least up to now.

The next time you hear a hushed whisper about the ecology of a woodland pond, or a marsh, or an area of capital W Wilderness or capital W Wildlife, remember this: Any ecological system is a stage in a battle, not even a pause or a truce in one, a battle that can be and often is pitilessly genocidal. Sometimes, in some places (when the climate or the geological conditions stay the same for a moment), there is a stalemate, for a moment (which may mean a few thousand years), and this is what we call an ecosystem. This can seem "good," and often very beautiful, though in nature there is no absolute "good," only systems whose forces balance each other for a while. Nature has no beloved children, only survivors, the ones she hasn't yet killed—not that she is *trying* to kill them, any more than she is trying not to.

Human beings, nature's most complicated accident, have already learned how to come within about fifty years of destroying a planet in two centuries. Learning how to transform it into a very pleasant (and permanent) place to live may take a little longer, but we certainly have the power and the brains to do it. And there are no other forces that we know of that can stand up to our power, intelligently used. We are by long odds the most powerful thing around. If we want to make something really superb out of this planet, there is nothing whatever that can stop us.

The destroying part was so easy we hardly had to think about it. Burn the forests, kill the buffalo, eat the tongue, and let the rest rot. Dynamite the fish. Bulldoze the land and then dump poisons over the blasted earth. Why worry? Isn't the land endless? You can always move west.

There is no reason why, for the first time, Mother Nature can't be told intelligently and authoritatively exactly what to do. She's only a set of rules, and we're learning them all.

Ecology can be planned. We can be the creative architects of ecosystems that will serve mankind, and protect the flora and the fauna that we *want* to protect, and that will surely be almost all of them.

For example, in *Silent Spring* there is a wonderful last chapter called "The Other Road," which outlines many steps toward a creative ecology. Ingenious methods are now being used by foresters, especially in Europe. New forests are carefully "inoculated" with birds, ants, forest spiders, and even soil bacteria. Modern forests don't have many old hollow trees, so nesting boxes are built for woodpeckers and other tree-nesting birds. Even owls and bats are brought in, so that the insect-hunting can be on a twenty-four-hour basis. Red ants are especially good at killing insects harmful to trees.

Ten thousand colonies of them have been introduced to ninety test areas in the German Federal Republic. Local schoolchildren look after the ants and the birds' nesting boxes. (Miss Carson didn't say how you look after an ant, but they do.)

Spiders are the best of all, and they are brought in by the thousands. A single spider in her lifetime can destroy (in addition to her own husbands) some two thousand insects. "A biologically sound forest has 50 to 150 spiders to the square meter." That's a lot of spiders.

In Canada sawflies are deadly to forests; they deposit their eggs in the needles of pine trees. The larvae drop to the ground and form cocoons. Men could go around and destroy each cocoon—but the Canadians have discovered a shrew (like a tiny mouse) that will eat up to eight hundred cocoons a day. Enter the shrews, exit the sawflies!

Miss Carson also cites a number of really dirty biological tricks played on insect pests, like the sterilizing of male screwworms, for a lot of nonproductive mating, and fooling gypsy moths with sex odors; they had the baffled gypsy moths trying to make love to chips of wood! And we all know about the recorded love songs of mosquitoes, leading love-sick males to electric grids. Insect viruses have been used, too, and wasps, deadly to the larvae of insects attacking apple trees.

These are all early steps in creative ecology. For decades we've used fish hatcheries to stock lakes and rivers. When the Great Lakes were linked with the sea, one result was that they were invaded by two pests from the sea, lampreys and alewives. Lampreys, nasty eel-like leeches, killed off many of the lake trout. The alewives, a kind of herring, came in such numbers that they were crowding out more useful fish. Creative ecologists developed a poison that killed lampreys; and they also discovered that salmon were very fond of alewives. Coho and chinook salmon were introduced to eat the alewives, and the people are eating the salmon.

Most of these examples are only partial remedies, a plugging of the dikes, a curing of symptoms. Some of them worked well. But often a partial solution, without a careful study of the whole ecology, can make things worse.

The Aswan Dam is a good illustration. The intentions were excellent: the area is arid, the people are poor. Dam the Nile, make a mighty reservoir, irrigate the whole area, and surely there will be prosperity! Thousands of people worked for many years, and the dam was built—and now it is almost an ecological disaster. The rich silt that the Nile formerly carried in its yearly floods to the Egyptian farms is now deposited in the lake above the dam, and eventually will fill it up. The delta is shrinking, the fishing is reduced, and worst of all, there is a great increase in the disease bilharzia, carried by the waterborne snails in the irrigation canals. You have to be very careful when you play around with ecology.

What we'll have to come to, in the future, is completely planned ecologies. A great deal of thought has gone into this already. There's even a name for it: the new science of *systems ecology*. I predict that a mountain of books will be written about it in the next decade. One of the early ones is called *Systems Analysis and Simulation in Ecology*, edited by Bernard C. Patten.[1] The first of two volumes is more than six hundred pages long. The object, ultimately, is to lead to "optimal design and control of ecosystems."

So man-made ecology is on the way. It has to come. And we shall consider, as this book does, things like "algal growth, isopod energetics, and fish predation models."

I think of the great six-hundred-page first volume, compiled by an army of serious ecologists, about a science I thought I'd invented. And when I read terms like algal growth and isopod energetics, I can hear, from somewhere, the sound of silly voices.

"What was that again? What are you reading?"

"It's right here—it's talking about the radiocesium movement through forest floor arthropod populations."

"Is it? Did you ever lie on the pine needles of a forest floor?"

"That's not relevant, really."

"What kind of nature would he make, I mean, a man who talks about the radiowhosit movement on a forest floor. Would it look like a Bunsen burner?"

"They're also talking about the coexistence in the phytoplankton and the properties of the secondary succession model of the—"

"Would they make it smell of formaldehyde, do you think?"

"Leave out the phytoplankton and where are you? Maybe no oxygen."

"Would he hear the birds and smell the flowers?"

I suppose what the silly voices are saying is that once the Systems Ecology Board (printed forms, in quadruplicate, and absolutely tireless data input) takes over, we're going to have to make sure that every Eco-Board includes at least one lady in a floppy hat and tennis shoes who does watercolors of woodland streams. She may not even be allowed to *touch* a phytoplankton (at least not without filling in a printed form), but she'd have the inalienable right to say, "I *do* think that would look nicer over by the willow tree!" And they will *have* to listen, and maybe make a few harmless adjustments to the arthropods and a slight jiggle in the radiocesium movement. It mustn't ever fiddle with the ecosystem, but it is *very* important for it to look nicer over by the willow tree.

What I'm saying, I suppose, is that we'll have to become gods, of sorts. We'll have to make it work with intelligence, but gently, too, with love, with more love than old Mother Nature ever had. And a lot more brains.

We already have more power than the ancients could ever imagine for their gods. With this power must go responsibility—and tender care. We've already proved that there's no limit to what we can do to our poor old earth. There's no limit to what we can make of her, either.

With a lot of love and a little bit of luck, we can make her into a bloomin' queen!

4

WOULD YOU TRADE YOUR AUNT LUCY FOR THE BATWINGED HERON?

Or, Do you realize that for a sizable segment of the population, ecology is just something for the birds?

One thing we're going to have to take into consideration on our way to the future is that a lot of people don't want to go there that way.

These people feel that the dedicated whoops-a-daisy ecologist and wildlife lover would gladly, at the drop of a buttercup, fence you in—and ten thousand others like you—for the convenience and pleasure of seven moldy batwinged herons, who might even prefer to be someplace else.

"But Mother Nature *put* them there!" the eco-freaks (to use their term) will say.

"Mother Nature put me here, too, without askin', and you can tell her to put me back."

This movement is bigger than you think, and one of its most vociferous spokesmen is Richard Neuhaus, who allows that nature is certainly okay in its place.

However, he is the pastor of a Lutheran church in the heart of Brooklyn, where very little nature seeps in, and where there are an awful lot of people. Neuhaus wrote *In Defense of People*, and his point is that we are part of the biosphere, too, and let's not forget it.

Neuhaus and his ilk rise up in righteous wrath when they hear some heiress in her Abercrombie & Fitch moccasins say that the national parks are simply being *ruined*. "By whom?" you ask. "By all those *people*, my deah!" It used to be, of course, that only *her* kind of people could get there. "But now, my dead, it's simply a swarming mob! And all those ghastly trailahs!"

This attitude is known in some circles as the "Sierra Club mentality" or "Keep the wilderness wild," by which they mean (some feel), "Keep it the private preserve of Our Kind of People, and the rest of you please leave quietly, and pick up those sandwich bags."

It goes back, says Neuhaus, as far as Henry VII (my guess is as far back as the pharaohs of Egypt) when wildlife was protected from the people, who wanted to eat it. (This was to some extent understandable, since it was all they had to eat.) It was protected so that the aristocrats could hunt it for sport (and eat it, too, of course).[1] The mantraps and the floggings of poachers are pretty rare now, but game is still raised and protected on the vast estates of the rich—protected, of course, so that it can be shot by the Right Kind of People. But not shot enough so that it can't be shot again next year.

"We were just seven guns, old boy, and we shot

four hundred and seventy-eight brace. Not bad, eh?"

(The odds are pretty good that he is a supporter of the Wildlife Fund. What's wildlife for, anyway?)

And René Dubos has written that "some of us are forgetting that ecology is for people. The ecology of city streets is as important as the ecology of the wilderness."[2] *More* important, say the antiwilderness boys.

Now, most people *are* wilderness lovers; that is, they would love to be able to break away more often from that commute and nibble on a bite-size chunk of wilderness. Others, *dedicated* others, not just the ah-wilderness-as-long-as-it's-mine folks, really do care. Let's suppose you're one of them, desperately concerned over the fate of the vanishing batwinged heron, and you need the vote of one of Richard Neuhaus's Brooklyn neighbors:

"We're terribly concerned," you say, "about these poor birds. They may die out."

"Well, yeah, we wouldn't want that to happen, huh? What kinda boids?"

"The lovely batwinged heron."

"Like a duck, huh?"

"Only more so, yes. We think there are only eleven of them left. They're living on this lovely wilderness marsh—"

"Yeah, I went to a wilderness oncet, out to the end of the BMT, and you know what? Coney Island!"

"For this you'd have to go farther."

"How? Walk?"

"If they turn this lovely marsh into a beach—"

"A beach, yeah? How big?"

"It's a mile and a half of coastline."

"For eleven ducks?"

You can see that there's quite a sympathy gap here, difficult to bridge even by, say, a fifteen-dollar book of photographs taken by Prince Philip, the Duke of Edinburgh, which might be long on ducks and short on people, and not likely to be sold on newsstands in Flatbush. This isn't meant to suggest that anybody likes ducks more than people.

Nor is it meant to suggest that Richard Neuhaus and his friends are against the batwinged heron, or any other kind, or that all marshes should be turned into beaches. But who knows? In some cases the birds might be happier with relatives, someplace else.

For those of you who are of the other persuasion, who don't want to be fenced in (you only want the other people to be fenced out), well, we've been conferring with our friend, the Nature Dastard:

"Nothing to it, old boy. If you want peace and quiet, you've got to keep the bastards out."

"How? Barbed wire?"

"Old hat, my boy. They can take legal steps! Make it a *Sanctuary*, boy! *Wildlife*, boy! See all that land?"

"Looks like a nine-hole golf course."

"Nonsense, boy! Prairie dog preserve!"

"I don't see any prairie dogs."

"And you won't, boy, little devils keep their heads down. Better had. Vanishing breed, you know. Worse than the whooping crane. Once this little oasis is overrun, you can say 'Bye-bye, prairie dog'! Marvelous thing, this ecology, boy. Keep the Wilderness! Up the Wildlife! And keep the bastards out, boy!"

In any case, if we're going to get to the future together, and in one piece, we're going to have to convince some of the people, especially the ones who live in the city centers, that ecology isn't simply an upper-class way of changing the subject, or even a lovely woodland path leading us as far as possible from the cities and the need to do anything about their problems.

Fake, people-baiting ecology can become just an escape mechanism, and even worse, it can hurt true ecology, and that will hurt us all.

5

"HOW MANY PEOPLE DO WE NEED?"
"HOW MANY CAN WE STAND?"

Or, How to use "population"
against people

Probably the most chilling of all the doomsday prophecies are the ones about the population explosion. Of course, this may be simply because they have a point—unless we're very careful.

On the other hand, there seems to be quite a lot of suspicion about some of these warnings. Do some of these Cassandras have an ax to grind? Are some of them really against people—at least the *common* people? Our Brooklyn friend, Richard Neuhaus, thinks so, and so does John Maddox in his *Doomsday Syndrome*. And I think so.

Certainly the first man to become famous for his alarming cry of "Population!" was very much anti–common people. The French Revolution had just exploded across the Channel, and Thomas Malthus, an English aristocrat, was upset. In 1797 he wrote his first

Essay on the Principle of Population. The Malthusian theory was that people increase by multiplication, and food more or less by addition, so that people are inevitably going to run out of food. Therefore, things can only be leveled off by starvation, disease, war, and "moral corruption." Malthus had a rather lip-smacking attitude about this. The people who were going to be leveled off weren't *his* kind of people; they were the poor, and it rather served them right, especially since they insisted on all that nasty fornication which he, Malthus, thought was simply frightful.

Malthus's geometric progressions haven't worked out. If they had, there'd be a dozen of us on every square foot of land in the world. But the real facts are not particularly comforting. World population by the time of the fall of Rome was about 400 million, reached 1 billion about 1600, 2 billion about 1900, and 3 billion by about 1950. It is now about 3.6 billion, will probably reach 4 billion by about 1980, and seems to be accelerating, with a possible total of 7 billion by the year 2000.[1]

It's easy to begin feeling a bit hysterical about all this, and many people have.

Two of the more excited books are Dr. Paul Ehrlich's *The Population Bomb* and William and Paul Paddock's *Famine—1975!*[2] Probably no doomsday book has scared people more, or sold more copies, than Dr. Ehrlich's. Is there a correlation here? He certainly pulled no punches. "The battle to feed all humanity is over," he wrote in 1967. "In the 1970's the world will undergo famines, hundreds of millions of people are going to starve to death in spite of any crash program embarked on now."

Well, we can now see that this is not going to happen. Thanks to the "green revolution," food production has gone up faster than population—which has not gone up as fast as Dr. Ehrlich predicted—and partly, we must admit, because people have been frightened by books like Dr. Ehrlich's!

As for the Paddocks' book, they predicted inevitable worldwide famine by 1975. Certain whole countries would have to be written off as hopeless and allowed to die. We would probably have to use the dread principle of *triage*, as practiced in battlefield dressing stations, when the wounded are coming in faster than the doctors can handle them. They're divided into three groups: those who can survive without treatment, those who will die even with it, and those who can be saved only if they're treated immediately. Only these last are treated; the mortally wounded are simply left to die. Apply this to the food problem, and you send nothing to the hopeless countries. They'll starve eventually, so why waste food? Which countries? Three named were India, Egypt, and Haiti.

Happily we didn't take the *triage* advice; the world is not yet a battlefield dressing station. No countries were deliberately left to starve, and no "hundreds of millions" did. (Hello India, Egypt, and Haiti! So glad you're still with us.) Biafra and Bangla Desh had a hard time, but in both cases it was war and not the worldwide food shortage that caused most of the trouble.

The people on the other side of the fence can go a bit far as well. Richard Neuhaus points out, as though it were pretty ominous, that *The Population Bomb* was published by the Sierra Club (and Neuhaus is sure they think redwoods are more important than people). And he's worried that some of the Carnegie Hall concert programs publicized the Ehrlich book with little cartoons of bombs, and the words "The population bomb keeps ticking." Does this, Neuhaus wonders, make the affluent concert-goer feel less guilty—to be sitting there listening to that affluent concert? And, he adds, wasn't the picture of the population bomb also on the matchbooks of an expensive New York restaurant, like Marchi's? Everyone eating in an affluent place like that should feel guilty—but having that on the matches makes them feel better!

There are still some pretty brutal points of view. Garrett Hardin, a professor of biology in California, feels that if the food of the world must really be shared, then America is lost, because the rest of the world is increasing much faster than we are. "Those who breed faster will replace the rest . . . in a less than perfect world, the allocation of rights based on territory must be defended if a ruinous breeding race is to be avoided." Is this a fancy way of saying, "Man the borders, boys! If any starving people try to get in, shoot to kill!"? Barry Commoner, who quotes Hardin in his

Closing Circle, remarks, "Here, only faintly masked, is barbarism."

If being scared titillates you, *I* can scare you, with solid figures. The most recent set I've seen are from Tomas Frejka, of the Population Council, and before that the Office of Population Research at Princeton, writing in the March 1973 *Scientific American*—and not *trying* to scare us at all. He says that "a continuation of the present [worldwide] growth rate (not to mention an increase in the rate) would bring the population of the world close to 7 billion around the year 2000, 14 billion in the 2040s and 28 billion in the 2070s." And that's more than seven times as many people as there are now.

In fact, Frejka points out, population is bound to rise rather sharply now, for a while, even if we *do* something about it, because medical knowledge is seeping into the developing countries, which were held down in numbers simply by a very high death rate. Nobody, or nobody *I* know, says we should stop that. Right now the expectation of life at birth in the developed countries is seventy years, and in many developing ones only forty.

The situation, especially in these developing countries, could become quite alarming. Frejka states: "If current fertility remains constant and mortality declines, the population of the less developed countries could be more than 10 times the present size by 2050."[3]

There are many who say, "Why worry? The world has room for lots more people. We can feed them all!" I agree that this can probably be done. We could possibly handle a world population of 35 billion, say, or some ten times the present number.

Shall we have a look at the happy people-full planet of the possible future?

Let 'Em Eat Beef!

Food is the main problem, but our technologists are already working that out. The ocean is full of plankton, and they're full of protein. There's fish farming, and there are always soybeans.

But technology is already moving farther ahead. For example, General Electric has just announced (*really!*) a new process for converting cattle dung into protein. Special bacteria are introduced; they consume the dung and form a protein mass, which not only gets rid of the stuff, but the protein is nutritious. GE suggests it could be added to livestock feed. It could, of course, be equally nutritious for humans, and in the years to come, when we have all those people, they'll have to eat something, won't they?

As they say on Madison Avenue, it's what we *think* things are that really counts. A junior copywriter, assigned to this account, might be instructed like this:

"Well, Harold, what we call it is Brochette de Vachette, and *we* know, and now *you* know, that it's actually cow dung. We push it mostly for snacks, a nice spread for crackers, and it makes a really tasty meat loaf. We're legally allowed to refer to it as 'a beef product,' which it assuredly is, no other form of dung is ever used, and we've cleared the phrases 'Vachette puts beef into you' and 'It's beef, through and through.' In fact, there's no question that it's been *all* the way through, is there, Harold?

"Take home one of the handy economy-size packs with you, boy, and try it out at home. Let the little woman see what she can make of it. It comes in our special biodegradable container with the picture of the smiling cow. Now you know why she's smiling, don't you, Harold?"

Hail the Potomaccolach!

The tomato and the potato will have to go. There won't be enough land for wasteful plants like that. All vegetables will have to do double or even quadruple duty. Botanists are really working on this now, developing a plant with edible roots, like the potato, and edible fruit, like the tomato.

In the crowded future we won't be able to stop there. The leaves will have to be edible, like spinach, and the stalks, like broccoli. And if flavor suffers, well, it contains vitamins, doesn't it?

"The problem was," the biologist said, "that the new potomaccolach biowonder vegetable was vulnerable to attack by a certain yellow beetle. However, one of our researchers, who had been eating nothing but potomaccolach for three weeks, went off the deep end and started eating the beetles. The rest, of course, is history!"

They're simply *crawling* with protein—and with just a little monosodium glutamate. . . ."

Hot Beds and Hot Lives

I'm convinced that we can *feed* them all right, but where will we *put* them all? Well, technology and a little thought can solve anything.

Some of the northern European countries, pretty crowded already, are importing workers from southern Europe to do the dirty work—Italians, Spaniards, Turks, and so on. Where can they all sleep? There aren't enough beds to go around.

The answer is the "hot bed" system: one bed for two passengers, the night-shift worker sleeping in the daytime and the day-shifter at night.

In our 35-billion future we'll have to expand this system; there's no use letting things sit around empty, the way we do now, is there? All facilities will have to service two or even three shifts every twenty-four hours:

"What a lovely little apartment, darling!"

"And it's all ours, every day, from six A.M. to two P.M.! Don't hurry your coffee, dear. We still have fifteen minutes."

"Where do you sleep?"

"We have beds right in 64B, just twenty-two stories downstairs, two lovely bunks, any time from ten P.M. to six A.M. So we come up here for breakfast."

And you'll be able to swim, or pedal a stationary

bicycle, or play isometric golf every day, though some people will have to do theirs on the 2:00 to 4:00 A.M. shift. What *is* isometric golf? Well—

Isometric Golf

Even today we have far too many people for golf, and it's really impossible most places to play the real thing unless you're either a millionaire or willing to get up at 4:30 in the morning (to get on the end of the queue of people who got up at 3:30).

This accounts for the success of the new electronic golf, or Golf-O-Rama, where the player hits his ball into a 9- by 9-foot screen, on which are projected still pictures of fairways at Thunderbird or Pebble Beach. A computer works out the details. This is now a reality —in fact, a commercial success—and the queues are beginning to form.[4]

Of course, when we have all those people, there isn't going to be room for any 9- by 9-foot screen, and certainly not enough elbow room to swing a club. Not for everybody, there isn't. After all, the object *is* exercise, and how much space do you really need?

"Darling, there's something in that closet!"

"I know, dear, it's Bertie. He's playing golf."

"*Golf?*"

"The new isometric golf. He just plugs himself in, sits there and ripples his muscles, and the computer tells him he's hooked it into the rough. It flashes a little picture on the tube."

So you see, there's no need to panic. We can always crowd them in and give them a good time.

But it is possible to cut down the population. The United States and Western Europe are already beginning to do it, and in fact have almost reached zero population growth. A figure in early 1973 showed that the United States was down to a fertility rate of 2.03—and the replacement level is 2.1.[5]

Certainly all the means to reduce birthrate are at hand for anyone who wants to use them, and in the near future there will be after-sex pills, once-a-month or even once-a-year pills or injections, male pills, and so on.

And the old deterrents to using them do seem to be decreasing. A survey made in late 1972 showed that four out of five American Catholic wives under twenty-five were using birth control methods other than the rhythm system.

For those who've had five boys while "trying for just *one* girl," or vice versa—well, predetermination of sex (coming any minute) will end all that. Just order one of each, if that's what you want, and *presto!*

The Rich and Happy Billion

So it isn't really necessary to eat cow dung or live on top of each other. Think about how things might be in the opposite direction, for a moment.

Wouldn't the future be much more pleasant if there were only about a third as many people as there are now? Just think of a third as many people on the beaches, in the camping grounds, on the ski slopes. Think of no more traffic jams or subway crushes. Do you really *want* to live in an anthill?

The problem of pollution would almost take care of itself. Nature could handle much of it unaided.

Imagine plenty of room everywhere, no worry that the suburbs of all cities will link up into one great reeking sprawl, with no open country in between. No problem of energy or running out of electricity when we need it most. No need for anyone to eat anything but the choicest, most succulent food, and plenty of room to grow it. Or would you prefer seaweed?

Would you like every city to be like Calcutta, or would you prefer your own acre of lawn or woods, or your own trout stream, swimming lake, or tennis court? And not just for Our Kind of People, but for all people on earth.

It's a choice we're entirely free to make. Nobody's pushing us to breed another 30 billion bodies in the next seventy-five years. Well, hardly anybody.

The population drop doesn't have to be sudden, just a gentle, leisurely decline in the birthrate over the next century or two, while we dabble with the rest of the solar system and cultivate the arts.

The rich and happy billion is something that is so completely possible and could be so delightful. Isn't it a shame that human beings seem to be psychologically quite incapable of considering it?

6

CATCH-23

Or, The Third World and
what you can do with it

Let's assume that you've been paying attention up to now and are becoming (if you were not before) a model citizen of the future world.

But what about that fellow next door? Nice guy, and certainly no villain. He's an earnest, hardworking American, driving himself into his third ulcer with selfless devotion, providing his loved ones with all the simple necessities of life—the third car, the new snowmobile, the automatic garage-door opener with the electric toothbrush and can-opener attachment, and the heated swimming pool.

He's poised for his next giant leap forward, moving up from the twenty-two-foot Wombat Supercharged Grand Prix 400-horsepower hardtop to the twenty-five-foot Double Supercharged 8-carb 550-horsepower Wombat GT. He wants to make sure his wife can make it all the way down to the shopping center and carry back that bag of groceries.

He's not a selfish man. In fact, he's a typically generous American:

GENEROUS AMERICAN: "I don't want it just for me! I want it for everybody! That's the whole point! Bring everybody up to Our Way of Life, the American Way of Life!"

"You mean, two cars in every garage? Heated swimming pools for everyone—Africans, Chinese, Indians?"

"Why not? Great for the GNP! Great for business!"

Well, why not, indeed? Why not share our wealth with everyone? Wouldn't it be good for them and also good for our business? It would be if, for instance, we had a series of empty neighboring planets, a few hours' flight away, all equipped with resources like the earth's. The facts are, however, that there's really no other place to go. And at the moment the United States, with about 6 percent of the world's population, is using up about a third of its resources, and doing about 40 percent of its pollution, and Western Europe isn't far behind.

According to that excellent Ward-Dubos United Nations report:

> An American baby, who will require a million calories of food and thirteen tons of coal a year during an average lifetime of 65 years, is going to run through the biosphere's available supplies at least 500 times faster than an [East] Indian baby looking forward to fifty years with an annual consumption of perhaps half

a million calories and almost no energy save what he
himself will produce from these calories.[1]

In short, if all the people of the have-not countries
(more than two thirds of the world's population) were
to be magically brought up to the American way of life,
as we're living it now, the world would end about a
week from Thursday.

Not only will the developing countries never be able
to live like this, but we won't be able to, either, unless
they keep on supplying us with their resources (especially their oil) to make all our wonders work.

And another problem is that the developing countries are beginning to find this out.

This leads to what I call Catch-23. Or, if we keep on
going the way we are now, we can't get there from
here.

Catch-23

Catch-23 is based on two basic assumptions of the
experts:

1. Population growth falls into three phases: (a) the
premedicine stage, in which the death rate and the
birthrate just about balance; (b) the medicine-aided
preindustrial stage: death rates down, birthrates boom-
ing, huge increase in population; and (c) the industrial stage, when population tends to stabilize. The
developing countries are now in the second stage, with
rapidly rising populations.[2]

2. But if these preindustrial countries become industrial, the planet can't support it.

So Catch-23 is: If the developing countries don't become industrial, their populations may go through the roof. If they do become industrial, the planet will go bankrupt. That is, unless we change things.

But how do we change things? Talk to them? Tell the developing countries they shouldn't have so many children? We've been doing this for decades, with very little success. Their attitude is "What business is it of yours? In the past you rich countries have always exploited us. Why should we trust you now?"

This understandable bitterness exploded internationally during the Conference on Human Environment held in Stockholm, Sweden, in June 1972. The industrial powers, hoping for quiet, obedient cooperation from the developing countries, were surprised and shocked to discover that the Third World was hopping mad. Iran, Algeria, China, and others were jumping up and down demanding "reparations" from the United States and other "imperialist powers" for inroads on world resources and crimes against the environment.[3]

True, the "Earthwatch" program was begun, with some 110 pollution-monitoring stations scattered around the world, but Anthony Lewis, of *The New York Times*, along with many others, mourned the fact that "nationalistic trivialities" took up most of the time.

Subsequently, a small fish was thrown to the Third World—the United Nations decision to set up environmental headquarters in Nairobi, Kenya.

This is, in fact, probably the number one problem of the planet—how to reach all of these people, how to give them better lives, and how to make them realize it is genuinely to their interest (and not just to ours) to have smaller families.

It is unquestionably in their long-term interest to do this. If the normal progression of their population continues, it will be they, not us, who will be the first to starve, though we shall have to do our best to feed them.

The problem is to make it clear that it is in their short-term interest, also, to do this.

Families in the United States and in Western Europe are smaller because it is now to their personal advantage to be smaller. In advanced industrial countries offspring must be maintained in higher education until almost middle age. Dwellings are scarce and expensive. It's simply more sensible to have smaller families.

In the developing countries children are cheap farmhands, and a kind of guarantee of support in old age. These countries have always lost a high percentage of their children; the rule seems to have been "Keep having them as fast as you can; you never know how many will live." Today, Frejka says, 95 percent of the children born in industrial countries reach the age of twenty, whereas in the developing countries only 60 percent live that long. Better medical care will raise that percentage (and the population), but a way of life will take longer to change.

Perhaps the best hope is education. India, for example, has a very ambitious plan to reach all the villages by satellite television (more about this later), and one of its objectives is to advocate and teach family planning.

China apparently has already gone a long way in this direction. One of their methods is simply to encourage later marriage. Somehow, that seems to me to be a reduction in the quality of life! Control is so much more pleasant than abstinence.

We shall have to keep trying to help the Third World. And if the Good Guys can't do it, the Bad Guys will. For instance, my old friend, the Future Dastard, says it's no problem at all:

"You're doin' it the hard way, boy!"

"There's an easier way?"

"Just keep 'em primitive, shiftless, and contented."

"How do you do that?"

"Reverse advertising, boy! Unboggle their minds!"

"Unboggle?"

"Boggle 'em down, boy! What we do here is boggle 'em up—make 'em want what they don't need! Down there, you boggle 'em down! Escalate the mañana! Make 'em not want the things they *do* need! Give 'em the Dropout Syndrome! Give 'em the hippie who-needs-it attitude. Send my son down there! That boy can make you drop out even if you never dropped in!"

"What about population?"

"Treat 'em like mosquitoes, boy! Send down five

million sterilized males, with guitars and raggedy clothes! Make love, not babies, boy!"

On the other hand, we could try to start setting them a good example, once we learn how to use people power. . . .

7

HOW TO USE PEOPLE-POWER

*Or, How to become a spare-time scourge
of public and private environment-busters*

It *is* true, as the doomsday people say, that we *can* pollute ourselves right off this planet. It *is* true that we can foul up the air and the water and our whole environment and make it so poisonous that our children and our grandchildren may never get to the future.

What is not true is that this is some kind of inevitable fate, a kind of ecological purgatory to punish us for our sins.

We can certainly control pollution. There are many ways to do it, and the first is personal. Everybody now knows all the rules of private hygiene against pollution. In the future these will have to become normal practice, like keeping our bodies and our clothes clean, like bathing or washing our teeth.

Where necessary, we will sort out rubbish, put rottable things on the compost heap, keep aluminum and steel cans for scrap collection, save paper for recycling, and so on. Already there are rubbish processing plants that do most of this automatically. We'll use nonpolluting soap powder (as soon as everybody decides what *is* nonpolluting) and buy products in biodegradable containers.

Future ages will regard today's dumping practices as we now do the medieval custom of throwing excrement out the window into the street. We'll simply become more civilized, and the sooner we reach this standard of personal cleanliness, the better.

But what about public cleanliness? Is there anything you can do if a company is dumping chemicals into your river, if a factory chimney is belching smoke into your garden, if a nearby town is pouring raw sewage into your swimming lake?

Yes, there is.

Did You Know That You Can Sue 'Em?

There are many grounds on which a private citizen, or a group of them, can sue polluters. People are doing it now, and many of them are winning. Some are even receiving considerable amounts of money in damages. More important, they're making polluters realize that fouling the environment can cost them money in the courts.[1]

You can sue simply on the basis of a "nuisance." You have a right to use and enjoy your property, and anyone who stops you is committing a nuisance. If you can prove financial or physical damages, you might collect money or get an injunction to require them to stop.

A variation of this, in common law, is trespass. You know you can keep unwanted people from trespassing on your land. Well, that's true of smoke or dust or gases, too, according to some courts.

How to Get Rich from the "Refuse Act"

New laws about pollution are being passed frequently—such as the new Federal Water Pollution Control Act. Even some of the old ones still have teeth. The old River and Harbor Act of 1899, called the Refuse Act, put fines of $500 to $2,500 per *day* on pollution, such as discharging refuse in navigable bodies of water. And note this, pollution sleuths: One half of the fine is to be paid to the person or persons who provide the information. Many people have collected on it, too.

Who Has a Right to Sue?

More and more people, and private groups, now have "standing," or the right to sue. It used to be that you had to be *personally* damaged before you had the right. In other words, if someone spoiled a scenic spot near you with a power plant or a pig farm, you couldn't sue because you couldn't prove personal damage. Now, in many cases, you can sue anyway.

For example, the Federal Power Commission told Con Edison it could build a hydroelectric project near a scenic and historical spot in the Hudson River Valley. Once upon a time, a private citizen would have had little say in such an affair, but this situation is changing. In this case, local people got together, called themselves the Scenic Hudson Preservation Conference, and the courts decided they *did* have a right to sue and to demand changes. The Sierra Club also won the right to sue in a similar case.

Some states are passing laws to this effect. Since 1970, any person in Michigan can bring suit against polluters.

One problem is that this can be very complicated. Whatever you may think of states' rights, or powers vested in local governments, all this division of authority is certainly rough on ecology. A randy little bit of raw sewage or an oxygen-hungry wall-eyed pike doesn't know when it's crossing a state line, or even a property line, and the problem doesn't end just because it's drifting into a new jurisdiction.

So you'll need good lawyers, idealistic Nader types, and bright, modern legislators, too, to find a way through the maze of laws, and, hopefully, to make some clearer ones and more uniform ones.

How to People-Power Corporations

Let's suppose that some company is blatantly dumping stuff into your river or fouling your air, and you *have* tried to sue.

"We've served the papers, it's all in the works," says

your crusading young lawyer, looking grim and tired.

"How long will it take?"

"The way things are going now, we might see some action in two or three years."

The problem is that the major tactic of corporation lawyers is *delay*. The way legal processes work, a good team of fancy lawyers can keep actions going for generations, from one appeal to another.

Is there a quicker way? Yes, there is.

You know all about the vast power of the "military-industrial complex" and the monstrous size of some corporations. Many of them have more wealth and power than some whole nations.

Can private people possibly have any effect on such giants?

They certainly can. There is nothing a big corporation fears more than your opinion—public opinion generally. You and enough others like you (and it could be far less than 1 percent of the people) could force any corporate giant, like General Motors or Standard Oil, to its knees in a matter of weeks. I know because I was in the marketing business for years. I was a vice-president of a big company. During the Joe McCarthy era I saw a mere handful of people make giants like some of my clients (including General Foods and Procter and Gamble) really tremble with terror. I saw how this terrible power could be used in an evil way. And believe me, it was evil. A handful of supermarket owners, by threats of boycott, were able to blacklist scores of good radio and television actors and writers and commentators on the basis of really ridiculous "guilt by association."

Unfortunately, the fear of this kind of power is one reason why so much sponsored entertainment in the United States can have little or no opinion or point of view. The advertisers are fearful of offending *anyone*, however stupid or prejudiced.

The point is that this is a kind of dynamite. It can be used in a good way, but only if it's used wisely and fairly. But it could save your life, or more likely the lives of your grandchildren.

Then what do you do about the company that's polluting your neighborhood? First, ascertain the accuracy of your facts; make sure the company is not doing the best it can to clean itself up. Sometimes this is a very complicated and expensive job. But once you're sure they need to be forced, then attack!

No need to march up and down, or break his windows, or anything crude like that. Remember this: The Achilles' heel of any company is the place where he touches the public, his ultimate customers.

Find out what his consumer products are, if any, and spread the word to all your friends and various organizations to stop buying them. Write letters to his marketing department, not poison-pen letters, but reasonable ones, and as full of hard facts as possible. "We like your products and would be pleased to keep on buying them—but we shall stop buying them unless you stop polluting our river."

Suppose, however, that like so many companies, it

doesn't make any product you can buy in a store. Suppose it makes steel, plastics, paper, or chemicals that it sells to other companies. Can you force such a manufacturer to behave, too?

You can, but unless you're accurate and fair, you'll be regarded as just another crackpot.

Let's say you're sure that XYZ Plastics is dumping stuff into your river. You've started legal action, you've written them nice but firm letters, and all you get is waffle and form letters and vague statements that the matter is under study.

Become a detective. It isn't very difficult. Find out who buys their plastics. Your friends, the business friends of your friends, or the people you know in the company itself may be able to tell you. You can even write them a letter on somebody's impressive letterhead, pretending to be a customer. As soon as you find out which consumer-goods companies buy his chemicals, you've got him. You will be absolutely amazed what an effect a few dozen letters can have—nice, level, honest letters like:

> The President [by name if you can find out, and why not?]
> Jiffy Container Corporation
>
> Dear Mr. ———:
> We like your plastic garbage cans and orange juice shakers very much, and hope to continue buying them. However, we know that the plastic used in your containers is made by the XYZ Chemical Company, which is now pouring seventy-eight tons of sulfuric

acid [or whatever, but be accurate; you may just have to go by a chemist's analysis of the water] into our river every working day.

We realize it isn't fair to blame you for this, and we're willing to give you a reasonable time either to (1) persuade the XYZ Company to stop this pollution or (2) obtain your raw materials from another company. If you help us, we shall be grateful, and we shall spread the word among our friends and organizations [list organizations if you can; the larger the consumer group you represent, the better] not only that you make superior products, but that you are interested in the public good.

If no steps are taken, we shall stop buying your products, and shall do our best to persuade our friends, neighbors, and fellow ——— members to do the same. We shall be grateful if you let us know what action you plan to take.

Sincerely yours,

Send copies of the letter to the president and to the head of the sales department of the chemical company, with a nice, level letter, stating simply what you have done. You will get a quick reaction. Steps will be taken very soon.

And remember, most companies and their executives are not villains. Companies have to make money to survive, but most managers know they won't be able to make it for long if they don't serve the public honestly and maintain its goodwill.

Every good public relations man knows that the best publicity is based on real public service, and the best public image a company can have is to create the impression it is somehow on your side, and it cannot long retain this image unless it genuinely is.

I don't think I ever met an out-and-out villain in all my years in business. Company managers are obliged to live on this planet, too, and they know it. They have to smell the same rivers, use the same lakes, and breathe the same air as the rest of us, and they have children and grandchildren. You may be surprised to discover after a pitched battle with some reluctant company that some of its executives, or at least junior executives, were privately rooting for you to win.

After all, what good is money, in any amount, on a stinking and dying planet? What fun is a pretty yacht if you have to moor it in sewage? Why have a nice sports car if you can only drive it from one garbage dump to another?

Many companies, as we'll see in the next chapter, are really on our side, and some are taking imaginative steps on their own. They have discovered this happy fact: Saving the earth is not only possible, it can even be profitable! And why not?

How to People-Power Politicians

Once you have learned how to people-power companies, you will find it relatively easy to people-power politicians.

Of course, the main object is to find a representative

who is on your side, though it is not always easy to tell. This is because politicians often face in two directions at the same time:

"How do you feel, Senator Blobb, about the problem of our poor river?"

"I'm with you all the way, friends! I'm an environment man myself, all the way!"

In fact, *no* one will ever say he is *against* the environment. But he may not really be with you *all* the way. He may also be facing the opposite direction:

"Have another Scotch, Senator! Frightful how expensive political campaigns are today! And we do need honest men like you, Senator. Now, about our waste disposal problem—"

"We must keep the river clean, suh!"

"Absolutely! But we need time to do it right, Senator! And some help from the government to do it!"

"How much time do you need, suh? You reckon ten years would be enough?"

Remember that a politician can face two ways at once, but he can *go* only one way. This leads us to a few simple rules:

1. Go by what he does, and not by what he says. You can tell by looking at his voting record.

2. Be careful of those speeches. He will be trying to show that he thinks the way you do, even when he does not. A really clever speech writer can, with the same speech, make the man who opposes you think the politician is for *him*, too. He may make you think he will clean up everything, regardless of cost, whereas the

man who should pay for most of it will believe that no matter what the cost, somebody else will have to pay it.

3. Let him know what organizations you represent, and the more the merrier.

4. Contribute to his campaign if you really believe he is honest. Any politician would much rather have a hundred contributions of five dollars than one of five hundred. A small contribution is a pretty sure vote.

5. If you don't like *any* of the candidates, propose one of your own. What about that young lawyer who's been helping you?

Should you vote only for the man who does exactly what you want? Well, only within reason.

Do you want him to have a mind of his own, or only a mind of your own? Be careful of a politician who spends *all* his time with his ear to the ground, who spends all his money taking polls and all his energies trying to outguess them. He may only be trying to find out what you want in order to seem to be giving it to you.

In fact, if he did only what you wanted him to do yesterday, the world would never reach tomorrow, but spend all its time trying to get back to yesterday. You would be chasing the tail of the past, which means you would really be chasing your own tail and going in circles.

The best politician will try to interpret today what you wanted yesterday in terms of what he honestly thinks will be best for you tomorrow. Otherwise why have representative government? This is why democracy is so complicated, and so interesting.

Do you know a better way?

SEVENTY-SIX TROMBONES AND
FIFTY THOUSAND Ph.D.'S
*Are the corporations doing anything
to save the earth?*

What are the huge corporations actually doing now to help save the earth? Many of these companies have vast research and development organizations, with laboratories worth hundreds of millions of dollars. More than fifty thousand scientific Ph.D.'s are working for them. What are they all doing?

One thing is certain: Every big company wants everyone to *think* it's doing something.

I wrote to twenty-eight of the biggest corporations, telling them I was doing this book and asking them if they had anything going that they wanted me to tell people about. The response was almost embarrassing. I'd estimate that on the average each one sent me material longer than this entire book. And there's no question that some of them are really doing a great deal.

Some I suspect are ecological monsters, telling the

publicity department to whoop it up about recycling the paper in the wastebaskets, while they're dumping a thousand tons of chemicals into the river every day.

Some of them act as though they'd hauled in the PR man and said, "Look, Joe, we gotta cook up something on this planet thing, huh?"

"Yeah, sure. Can I have something to go on? I mean, are we actually *doing* anything?"

"Look, Joe-boy, we hired you to make us look good! You want people to think we're just sitting on our tails on this whole doomsday thing? Howsabout you goose the employees' association to go on a litter drive, or something?"

So they bring out the brass bands and the mimeograph machines, and it looks almost as good as though they were doing something.

One company stated that it had 1,100 Ph.D.'s working for it, plus many thousands of others with lesser scientific degrees. A team like this should be able to reorganize the galaxy and make a nice profit doing it. However, my own experience with very large corporations not specifically with this one) would lead me to assume that of these 1,100, about 750 are spending their time in meetings and writing memos to each other, trying to change what they decided in the last meeting, or trying to take credit for it, or whipping up a strategy for the next meeting. Another 100 or so are waiting for someone to tell them what to do, and perhaps 200 more are redesigning the roto-widgit for the

Model 737 toaster, for the sole purpose of putting into the advertising the phrase that the 1976 model 737 toaster has a new double-whammy roto-widgit. This would leave about 50 to save the planet—and we would think that 50 really functioning Ph.D.'s could make a startling contribution. Then, where is it?

Other companies are being forced to do something *now*, by law, with definite standards and limits. The automobile companies are all in a state of shock, facing ruin if they don't meet the pollution requirements. There's no question in my mind that they wouldn't be working the way they are on special antipollution gadgets if they hadn't been pushed hard.

Right now they're at it in a frenzy. Ford says it has spent more than $360 million in five years on emission controls, and in the last year had more than 4,600 engineers and technicians assigned to the program. Both General Motors and Chrysler are working just as hard. GM, for instance, has actually tested almost every conceivable method other than bicycle pedals, including the rotary or Wankel engine, the stratified charge engine, and the intake valve-throttled engine, diesels, gas turbines, Stirling engines and steam engines, batteries, fuel cells, as well as various hybrids using both engines and batteries. They've sent me diagrams of them all. Though fascinating, there are no miracles, and so far no practical solutions that meet the requirements, and no certainty that they will be able to meet them even at the new, postponed (at this writing) date.

Using the gasoline engine, there seem to be two

major approaches: (1) to design engines with cleaner combustion (as Chrysler hopes to do with its CAS, or clean air system) and (2) to attach a catalytic converter to the exhaust pipe.

At this writing, the United States car companies have reduced hydrocarbon emission more than 80 percent, monoxide about 70 percent, and nitrogen oxides about 50 percent. That's a considerable accomplishment. However, the federal requirements for 1975, now postponed until 1977, are for a 90 percent reduction of both hydrocarbons and monoxide, and eventually a 90 percent reduction of nitrogen oxides as well (a year later, by the current plan).

It is embarrassing to everyone that two Japanese cars (Honda and Mazda) and a German one (the Mercedes diesel) can already meet the federal requirements.

General Motors says the car companies are *not allowed to pool their information on emission controls*— it would be against antitrust regulations! So you can see that rampant bureaucracy can foul up the air, too. Are we living in an insane asylum?

"Sorry, old boy," said the man in the Chevrolet to the man trapped in the burning Ford. "Love to help you, but the antitrust fellows wouldn't like it!"

The car companies are too busy with this crisis to worry much about really advanced future systems. Inevitably, as oil is used up, cars will run on energy produced by electricity, in turn generated by solar, geothermal, or nuclear power. And before that probably on fuel synthesized from coal. The electrical power will be carried around in batteries, ultimately some kind of high-energy density battery with many times the power per pound of our heavy lead-acid batteries.

Cars can now run on water—that is, water cracked by electricity. With the unlimited electric power that will eventually be available from thermonuclear fusion, all you need is water and you can make hydrogen, which can be bottled and burned, like gasoline, in engines. And what comes out of the tail pipe? Water vapor! Cars have already run on hydrogen, of course, but at the moment it's a bit awkward, because in liquid form hydrogen has to be kept very cold. So the technology will be difficult, but certainly not beyond our ability to solve. Who'll make the first commercially practicable hydrogen car? Shall we wait for Honda, Mazda, or Mercedes?

As to other save-the-earth work, Ford seems to be the most dedicated and energetic, with much progress in collecting and recycling junked vehicles. They've developed a new process for melting down and reusing polyurethane foam, the seat padding in most cars.

And what will the future cars look like? "Bigger and bigger!" say the safety people. They'll have to be, won't they, to get in hydraulic bumpers, the impregnable safety cage, the exploding air bags, the new inflatable safety belts, and all the various catalytic converters and pollution filters? But will the Nader Tank really run— or get better than five miles to the gallon?

"Smaller and smaller!" say the energy people, looking nervously at the foreign imports that use half as much gas, at a time when there's not enough to go around.

We may even have the inflatable car, one great air bag, able to hit anything, and just go *phooooph* like a beach ball. And it will have extra air capacity, to make it inflatable to double size—for parking in front of the country club.

The car companies are under the gun, and probably should be, but a great many others are doing fascinating work, pushed by nothing more than the desire to make money—and the realization that even money isn't going to be much good if we're all dead.

After reading good material fron Monsanto, Raytheon, General Electric, and Union Carbide, I'm not worried about garbage and rubbish pollution anymore. We can handle it. They've worked out systems of processing refuse that almost pay for themselves, and any city can have one put in. Those that don't are simply not paying attention.

Monsanto has a system called Landgard, and the company is building a big plant for Baltimore now. It will process one thousand tons of municipal waste a day, shredding it, baking it down to almost nothing (in enclosed furnaces, no smoke or fly ash gets out), separating out the residue, reclaiming metal and other usable wastes, scrubbing the gases, purifying the water, and so on. Systems like this *make* enough combustible gases to do the work. Union Carbide's system, similar to this, is, they say, 98 percent efficient and produces a fuel gas.

Raytheon is now constructing a full-scale operational plant for Lowell, Massachusetts. The pilot plant, which was built in collaboration with the U.S. Bureau of Mines at College Point, Maryland, has been processing 4 tons of refuse a day. When finished, it will take in 670 tons a day from the city incinerator, and each year should salvage 1,000 tons of aluminum, 700 tons of zinc and copper, over 20,000 tons of scrap iron, and so on. The plant is expected to pay its own way in recovered materials.

On a larger scale, General Electric is developing a system for all of Connecticut, recovering solid wastes and energy from some 7 million tons of refuse a year.

Almost all pollution problems can be solved technically if we take the trouble and spend the money to do it. We don't *have* to have that rising, exponential computer curve that leads to doomsday. In fact, IBM itself has computers working on this. (A computer will work in sensible directions or silly ones; it will do whatever you tell it to do.) IBM has put out a whole book on computer work in environmental science.

One study, for example, is a brain-shattering analysis of waste disposal and its relation to subsurface hydrology. What it's saying is that just burying waste or piping it in liquid form into holes in the ground (as some factories are doing) can be almost as dangerous as dumping it into the river, because it eventually mixes with the groundwater. So far, the IBM study shows, the best thing is sanitary landfill—carefully calculated to prevent seepage. Another IBM study examines the dispersion of smokestack effluents—or, exactly where does all that airborne pollution finally go?

And speaking of smokestacks, there's no need for any of that pollution. Monsanto, for one, makes smokestack-scrubbers, or "mist eliminators," with fiber-glass filters that remove chemical pollutants. One of its clients not only removed his mercury mist, but recovered thirty thousand dollars' worth of mercury every year (and the planet is very short of mercury). Du Pont, too, makes these stack-scrubbing systems.

There's no excuse at all for pollution of lakes and streams, either by sewage or by industrial chemicals. The organic nutrients in sewage can be processed into fertilizer, but one problem is the reduction of the oxygen in the water. Union Carbide has a system called Unox, already in use, which generates oxygen and forces it into solution in the water. This is more efficient than aerating water, because the nitrogen in the air gets in the way of the oxygen transfer. For chemical pollutants in the water, Carbide has developed an obsorption system based on a molecular sieve; it eliminates nitrogen oxides, sulfur oxides, and mercury emissions. All this is highly technical stuff, but they're highly technical problems. Westinghouse, Monsanto, and Boeing are all doing good work in water purification.

The doomsday people are frantic about the energy problem, because we're using up all the fossil fuels, especially oil, which will all be gone in a few decades.

Futurists have written off oil already. It was a temporary expedient.

But the companies are doing more work on energy now than on anything else. We still have enough coal to last a few centuries, but coal can pollute, especially coal with a high sulfur content. However, Westinghouse, together with the Office of Coal Research, is working on a commercial plant near Terre Haute, Indiana, to convert high sulfur coal into clean gas that can be burned without pollution, as in electric power plants. General Electric and others are doing coal gasification work, too, removing the sulfur and making clean-burning gas.

But even when the coal is gone, we don't need to be without energy. More power than we use now comes every day from the sun, and many companies are working on ways to use it. Honeywell, for instance, is in the midst of a solar energy project with the University of Minnesota and the National Science Foundation, studying reflectors, heat pipes, and storage facilities. And two astronomers, Aden and Marjorie Meinel, at the University of Arizona, have devised a solar power farm covered with steel pipes coated with a special optical substance, and filled with heat-retaining chemicals for generating heat, to make electrical power.[1]

Comsat, the satellite company, has developed improved silicon solar cells, 30 percent more efficient than the old ones. Their original object was simply power for their satellites, but Dr. Peter Glaser, of Arthur Little, Inc., suggests using solar cells in a giant power satellite with twenty-five square *miles* of them, sending electrical energy to earth by microwave! One such satellite, they estimate, could power all of New York City. A GE scientist, commenting on this scheme, wasn't dismayed by the size of the satellite, but thought there might be a few wrinkles to iron out before that kind of power could be sent by microwave.

There is almost unlimited heat and power within a few miles of every home and factory—straight down. It's geothermal, the earth's heat, the thing that makes volcanoes hot. In some places it comes to the surface, as in hot springs, and some of this is now used for power, but that's a microscopic percentage of the enormous amount available. The Atomic Energy Commission suggested setting off atomic explosions deep in the earth and pumping water into the cavities of rubble created. The resulting steam would generate power. Conservationists were frightened by this, and so am I. They'd certainly have to be *very* careful. So far, I've heard of no corporation that is exploring this geothermal source of power.

But most companies are betting on nuclear power, and many are working on it. Perhaps the most spectacular plans are from Westinghouse, which is now building the first large-scale breeder reactor at Oak Ridge, Tennessee. This is the new kind of atomic power plant that transforms rather scarce U-235 into plutonium—meaning that it literally "breeds" new fuel as it goes along. It could multiply our nuclear fuel reserves by perhaps seventy or eighty, and, say Ward and Dubos, "could power the world for another millennium."[2] But we must still solve the problem of what to do with all the radioactive waste.

Westinghouse is also building a nuclear plant in the Atlantic Ocean, about twelve miles from Atlantic City, New Jersey. It will be floating, moored behind an enormous breakwater. Being out there should reduce possible danger and also thermal pollution.

Everyone knows that we'd have unlimited power if we could make it the way the sun does, by nuclear fusion, the power of the hydrogen bomb. This is clean power, but the problem has been to construct a "furnace" that will hold heat at a temperature high enough to vaporize anything. "Well, anything," the physicists said, "except magnetism," and for years they've been trying to construct a mighty magnetic "bottle." Many have been built already, in laboratories, but at this writing there is no practicable power plant. The *Scientific American* estimated some years ago that the odds were pretty good that one would be working in a decade or two.

However, a newer and possibly more promising way was devised by Dr. Moshe Lubin, of the University of Rochester, and the Oak Ridge National Laboratory. Suppose, thought Dr. Lubin, you make a very tiny hydrogen bomb explode in a bath of liquid? Take a very small hollow pellet of deuterium-tritium and drop it into a whirlpool of molten lithium inside a pressure vessel. Then all you have to do is vaporize the pellet. A few years ago there would have been no possible way to do this, but just in time the laser has come along. You can hit the pellet with a violent blast from a laser pulse, and this should create the miniature hydrogen bomb, actually making the pellet give off neutrons and heating the lithium enormously, creating vast power, and from it electricity.

A great deal of effort is going into this, to make it into a practicable source of energy. General Electric, for example, is collaborating with the University of Rochester to develop lasers powerful enough to heat the deuterium pellets to 100 million degrees.

At this writing, however, there is still no workable fusion power plant. My prediction: If there isn't one by the time this book is published, there is at least an even-money chance that we'll have one within ten years—and a 90 percent certainty within twenty years. If the two possibilities above prove to be unworkable commercially, we'll think of others, because the principle of power from fusion is known and is sound. It's just a matter of very complex mechanics now, but complex mechanics are what we humans can handle best.

So, though energy is almost certain to be our biggest crisis in the short term—it is at the moment—it will not be (like population, pollution, and raw materials) a continuing, perpetual human problem. It will be solved. Future man will have (if he gets that far) all the power he can use.

With a great deal of electricity, made in huge fusion or breeder plants, one problem will be to transport it, in quantities much greater than before, into city centers, where it will supply *all* power, for heating, transportation, and vastly increased electronic equipment. Moving large quantities of electricity over wires, even high-tension wires, is very wasteful, and the farther it's carried, the more wasteful it is. What, then, is the new, future way to transport electricity? It's cryogenic; if your power cable is very, very cold, the electricity flows through it almost without loss, like a bobsled sliding down an icy run.

Many companies are experimenting with this. Union Carbide is using liquid helium to super-chill cables made of niobium, and they have a capacity as high as 10 *billion* watts, or some twenty times the capacity of today's transmission lines. GE is doing similar work with a cryogenic aluminum cable, chilled to $-320°$ F., and this cable has handled up to 450,000 volts.

Westinghouse is working on "frozen electricity," too. The company has built a 5-million-watt experimental generator whose heart is a spinning electromagnet refrigerated to $-452°$ F. It is much more efficient than ordinary warm generators.

Therefore, it seems likely that in the future we'll be getting "cold" electricity, through refrigerated cables. No need to worry, though, that your kilowatts will arrive frozen stiff, like Birds Eye peas. They'll fry your morning eggs as quickly as the old kind.

And speaking of generators, once we achieve controlled thermonuclear fusion, we probably won't need generators at all. The process can make electricity directly, without going through steam turbines, generators, and so on, losing power all the way. As Ward and Dubos explain: "The stream of particles—electrons, protons, helium ions—released from the plasma by accelerated neutrons bombarding the deuterium would pass through a series of magnetic fields at decelerating speeds; electrons would then be diverted and positive ions collected in such a way as to pass into direct current without going through an intermediate steam-powered generator."[3] Or, to put it into my language: instant electricity!

And even before we get to thermonuclear fusion, we'll make electricity directly from the combustion of normal fossil fuels, by MHD, or, as we fellows call it for short, magnetohydrodynamics. This uses a very hot high-velocity stream of ionized gases and can make electricity with about one third less fuel than our old generating processes. We Americans don't have one working yet—at this writing—on a commercial scale, but the Russians do; they've been lighting parts of Moscow with an MHD generator for a couple of years now.[4] We used to lead the world in things like this. What's happened?

In mass transportation our big corporations are doing some work, though we're certainly behind the Japanese and even the Europeans in this area. The villains have been mainly the doddering American railroads. Back in the 1950s Ford built an experimental model of an air-cushion tracked vehicle, and in the early 1960s Westinghouse proved that a magnetic-suspension vehicle would work. No railroad showed any interest.[5]

Today there are a number of other interesting projects. Bendix put up an experimental "guideway" system at the Transport Exposition (Transpo 72)—little automatic electric cars that run by themselves, almost like electric elevators. You just get on and press the button for your stop, no motorman or conductor required. This, of course, is for transport within cities.

Boeing has carried this a step further by building a complete PRT (personal rapid transit) system at Morgantown, West Virginia, where the university's campus, scattered around the city, was almost completely bogged down by traffic jams. This system, sponsored by the Urban Mass Transportation Administration, has overhead concrete guideways and completely automatic electric cars, requiring no drivers. Half-hour trips from one campus to another are reduced to five minutes or so. With such systems, all automobiles could be kept out of the city center and people would move about much more quickly and with no pollution.

There are a great many other, varied projects under way in research and development laboratories. A.T.&T.'s incredible Bell Laboratories, inventors of the transistor, are working in many directions. One of their most recent is an ingenious way of measuring nitrogen oxide air pollution, perhaps the most dangerous component of car exhaust, by using laser beams interrupted by a rotating shutter and fired through an air sample. They can identify quantities as small as ten parts in a billion. They're also working on car exhaust filters and have developed crystals made of manganese and cobalt and other rare earth elements that seem to work better than the expensive platinum catalysts.

The most amazing of General Dynamics' numerous projects is a proposed submarine oil tanker that could transport 170,000 tons of oil from the Alaskan north slope *under the ice* to the forty-eight southern states. This was intended as an alternative to a pipeline, which some ecologists thought would be dangerous. Latest word, however, is that we'll build the pipeline.

Another far-out project already in use is Bendix's development of multispectral photography and analysis, or taking pictures using the many parts of the spectrum, from ultraviolet through far infrared. Vast amounts of information have already been obtained by using this kind of photography from high-flying planes, and especially from satellites, showing crop damage, pollution, availability of new resources, and so on. Polaroid, too, has been doing work in this area. This kind of photography should be invaluable in our exploration of space, particularly with unmanned probes. And besides that, some of the pictures are strangely beautiful, gloriously colored new views of the planet.

Some companies surprise us with work that seems, at first, almost unrelated to their products. We can expect that a company like International Paper would be deeply involved (as they are) in massive reforestation projects and experiments in developing new kinds of super-trees—but would you expect it of U.S. Steel, which has planted millions of trees over once-mined areas? Today Steel manages forest lands more than twice the size of Rocky Mountain National Park.

And one of the most concerned companies in America is Xerox, doing massive public relations about the environment, with television programs, books for children about making toys out of old containers, much study of paper recycling, and a superb new $3.5 million sewage and waste disposal system for its main factory town, Webster, New York.

Polaroid is equally conscientious. The company had such frightful guilt complexes about all those instant negatives that people were scattering around our beauty spots that they loaded all their instructions with pleas: "*Do* be careful about dropping this negative!" It wasn't enough, so a major design requirement for their new camera was that *no* residue whatever should be left over—and there wasn't.

Much of the company puffery, of course, can be discounted. A favorite trick is one I call piggy-back riding—the massive, dramatic advertisement or stockholder report that goes like this:

BLASTOBAMCO TO THE STARS!
(Full-color pictures of a moon-rocket takeoff! Astronauts dangling in space by umbilical cords! The blue and white earth, from space!)
Copy: The Blastobam Company has done it again! Once again to the moon! And Blastobamco onward to the stars!

And much more. You'd think the entire Blastobam board of directors was in the command module. And every actual word in the ad is true. Blastobam did, indeed, go to the moon. They're the people who make that plastic washer on the orange juice container that the astronauts use, and all systems were always "Go!" They even explain this in the small print at the bottom.

But generally, it's encouraging to see how much work is being done. If all the companies were doing as much as some of them—like Bell Labs, Westinghouse, GE, and Monsanto—then we might be able to have economic growth and a richer quality of life as well.

America probably still leads the world in technology, but the lead is becoming smaller and smaller. The Western Europeans, the Japanese, and the Russians are all growing faster than we are in research and development. At the present rates, we're certain to lose our lead.

But the competition is healthy. What the others are doing to help save the planet will certainly help us, as well.

There is no harm in making it profitable to preserve the earth. But a great many of us will want to do our best to do our share regardless of profit, even regardless of cost.

9

YOU AND ME AND THE GNP

*Or, Our gross national product and
what we can all do with it*

Before we leave those companies altogether, we really should say a word, or perhaps even have a moment of silence, for the GNP.

The gross national product index has become the laurel wreath, the flapping banner, of the modern industrial world. It is, they say, a kind of totalizer, the final end result, one number that says what we all did last year.

Ask anyone who matters how well any country is doing, and he will know, because he knows its GNP, and he will tell you. It is why the Japanese yen has been going up, and our yen, or dollar, has been going down —their GNP is going up faster than ours. It is why you will have to pay more for that Toyota.

If you're one of those people who say, "Once you've got a GNP index, what can you do with it?" well, then, listen. "Will it really make us happy," you say, "if we raise the GNP? Should we do everything we can to raise it?"

Well, almost everything. There are all kinds of steps you can take. For instance, one thing is to jam on your brakes, right in the middle of the New Jersey Turnpike (or the turnpike nearest to you). The car in back of you will hit you, and the car in back of him will hit him, and so on for twenty or thirty cars. This may, of course, kill you, but it will certainly raise the GNP. The money that comes into the car repair garages is part of the GNP, and if some are total write-offs, that means new ones, and more "P."

If there are broken legs or fractured skulls—well, hospital income is part of the GNP, to say nothing of all those insurance adjusters (their salaries are part of it) and the funeral parlors and even the coffin makers. It's all in there. In one second of concentrated thought you might raise the GNP half a million dollars. And it's something any of us could do.

In fact, the GNP includes just about anything that happens, and it doesn't have to be all forward motion. I have my own apparatus for electrical prediction and can show you how it will work, on a kind of exponential basis. For the benefit of the Club of Rome, I've plugged in my special systems dynamics typewriter (220 volts, with repeating hyphen) and have analyzed the various subsystems, sitting always in a calculating position, facing directly toward Cambridge, Massachusetts, and M.I.T.

I've done a new world model of a projected year,

1979, with special reference to the American GNP. All the feedback loops are preserved in a ·safe place in the file, along with the crisscrossing curves (often vertiginous). Anyone who is interested, and not afraid to face facts, can examine them. Everything is written in my own computer language, called *English*. The result of it all is a "scenario" (as Herman Kahn would say), and from that I've distilled the following paragraphs.

1979: A Dynamic Projection, GNP-wise

No one could have guessed, at the beginning, just how far 1979 would go, in addition to going as far as 1980. All the economic indicators, car loadings, electrical power production, steel, and so on, were poking along at about normal rates.

However, a number of factors (rather easily predictable from the old computer printouts, but no one noticed) began to operate. For one thing, the winds began to rise, just enough to blow the roofs off houses, but not (luckily for the GNP) off the factories. The whole roofing industry began to light up, bringing along with it nails and steel production, ladders and therefore timber, and hospitalization (people falling off the ladders, and people without roofs catching bad colds).

The GNP in April (the winds were mostly in March) was up several points, the Dow Jones was beginning to go through the roof (in a purely metaphorical sense, since the roof of the New York Stock Exchange was unaffected).

The general euphoria was contagious; the dictators of fashion decided the moment was ripe to change "the look," and did so, drastically, to the small waist, or hourglass, look. There was resistance, but not for long. Soon 50 million women had to have corsets, and 500,000 workers were rushed into the factories to make them. At prices averaging $100 a corset (the construction was complicated) this added $5 billion to the GNP, to say nothing of all the new dresses, and the usual spin-off, cars to corset makers and so on.

Every economist knows that one thing leads to another. For example, General Motors, which in 1979 was getting out monthly, rather than yearly, models, rushed into production (for its July model Oldsmobile) a special Hourglass GT, with a definite chrome and vinyl pinch in the middle. This made it only slightly more uncomfortable for rear-seat passengers. (Geneticists were already trying to breed people with shorter legs, for rear-seat passengers.) It sold well, in pastel colors, to women buyers.

The tight corsets also led to constriction of female livers, kidneys, and other more exclusively female organs, resulting eventually in disabilities, separate bedrooms, and, predictably, distraught husbands.

For example, one husband, whose wife was of a most fashionable shape, but almost completely out of action, happened to be a demolition contractor. Hired to tear down some old buildings, he was so upset that he dynamited an entire new housing development.

This sort of thing was repeated everywhere, and

since all of the spoiled material had to be replaced, the GNP increased enormously. Everything was up. Commodities were never higher, including the Chicago Futures, from soybean oil (unbelievable!) to frozen pork bellies. The Dow Jones hit 2200, which is almost boiling point, and by the end of the year the final GNP index was up 18 percent, or just 1 percent under the 19 percent rise in Japan, which had managed to avoid all these calamities.

All the people in the United States agreed they had never spent a more miserable year.

Of course, no one can claim that the GNP index caused these unfortunate events; it merely measured them. Simply stopping the index would change little and would make idle all those people who spend their lives totting it up. What else would they do?

Let us have one, by all means, and keep it in one corner of the financial page. Anyone who wants it can find it.

The Case for the Pleasure Index

We do need an index that really means something, and you can call it whatever you like—the Jolly Level, the Whee Rating, or the Wow-Jones Index. It must be a carefully (and very seriously) calculated index of the quality of life.

No country really has one yet, but one company has taken a step in that direction, a firm that, oddly enough, makes automobile tires primarily. The *Michelin Guide*, which began in France but is now expanding to cover all of Europe, has been carefully, even scientifically, testing and measuring many aspects of the quality of life.

Scores of Michelin inspectors spend their lives tasting wines and sniffing cheeses and savoring sauces, even taking careful note of the delights (if any) of the location, the view, and the general ambience of hotels and restaurants and resorts. The really *pleasant* places they put in red, and indicate the spot from which you can see the loveliest view.

The Michelin men are all very serious, utterly incorruptible, and their standards are precise. After all, what is more important than the enjoyment of life? Let a restauranteur water the sauce, refrigerate the Camembert, fail to cool his *vin blanc*, or to *chambré* the *rouge* —and *wham!*—the man from Michelin will lower the boom, or, to be specific, will simply remove the little rosette from his listing, or even, in case of mortal sin (like saying the wine is included in the price, if it is not), he will remove the listing. Henceforth his customers will only be those with last year's edition. The *Guide*, needless to say, accepts no advertising.

This attitude, being as serious about the enjoyment of life as we have been about the GNP index, must become universal. And it must include far more than the wines and the sauces and the views. The pleasure-inspectors everywhere (and they must *be* everywhere) will be men and women with a delicate sensitivity to the fragrance of the air, the clarity of the water in the brooks, the pools, and the lakes, the plumage and the songs of the birds, the quality of the brass band, the smiles in the public parks, the tone and the pulse of the university—not only its academic excellence but the amount of mental pleasure and sparkle it brings to heads of all ages in the town.

It won't be easy, for example, to rate Toledo over Knoxville or Indianapolis on so many facets of the quality of life: the tone of public whistling, the twinkles in the eyes, the slipperiness of the slides in the playground or the swingability of the swings, the taste of the tap water, the quality of the bread and the beer, the scent of the blossoms, the beauty and the bounce of the girls. A final decision could hinge on a string quartet, a few extra lilac bushes, a fine actress in the town theater, or a lovely mural on an empty wall.

Naturally, cities will compete in pleasure ratings. City—or even state—governments will rise or fall on good or bad ratings. A good rating will be good for business, but even better for the people.

It might even raise the GNP, but nobody would mind.

10

COMMUNICATIONS: THE UNTOUCHABLE WONDERS

*Or, How to keep people from a future
that's already in the past*

I have a feeling this is going to be the angriest chapter
in the book. I spent my whole business life in the midst
of radio and television broadcasting and left years ago
with the usual mixture of sorrow, frustration, and rage.

We are all being walked over, bamboozled, and
swindled out of a heritage. We have built an incredible
playhouse and forum and fountain of knowledge as big
as the whole earth, and we've filled it with spit and
garbage.

And there *is* something we can do about it. We are
going to have to make it a strong political issue. It is not
enough to have a little committee sitting over at the
Federal Communications Commission. We are going to
have to elect representatives to give the air to us—the
citizens—even if we have to pass amendments to the
Constitution to do it.

We need the air, and the space above the air, and the ground under it, because now we can use them all. The wonders of our electronics are bound to increase and multiply, but at this moment we have the technical know-how to do almost anything we can imagine. The only thing stopping us is a monstrous tangle of political and corporate red tape and finagling, all of it ever so legal. Legal means laws, and in a democracy laws can be changed by the people, by us.

What can be done now, using today's technology, has been outlined by Peter Goldmark,[1] the wide-ranging genius who invented the long-playing record, a color television system, and about 158 other things. He was for many years head of the CBS laboratories.

The main key to the wonders, says Goldmark, is broad-band communication, which includes cable television. We're now using, in more than 5 million homes already wired for cable TV, the old coaxial cable, which can carry about a thousand times more information than a telephone line. And we already have wave guides, hollow tubes that can hold many times that, and in experimental form flexible glass-fiber channels, or "light pipes," through which lasers can haul an almost infinite amount of electronic bits, enough for thousands of television or phonavision channels.

But let's go back to the old Model-T coaxial cables. Here is what is technically possible today, has been possible for years, and is probably as politically and bureaucratically impossible now and for perhaps decades to come as would be a weekend on the dog star. You could have twelve or more television channels, even including local TV, which comes in only over the wire, and some that could be piped in from anywhere, say, the BBC, or television from satellites, piped directly from the system's ground antenna to you; also, a professional TV channel especially for you, if you're a doctor or a public official; educational channels to which you could react or respond; a printer which could give you the daily paper or sports or market results, or even print out personal letters to you; a "frame grabber" which will make an instant print of any image on the television; access to special programs, such as a championship fight or game or a Broadway first night.

The two-way facility would enable you to order things from a store, perhaps directly from a shopping program, which would show you the items; take part in public opinion polls, or give your opinion (thumbs up or down) on the program you're watching; be warned of fire or burglary; have meters read; or even be able to make sure (if you're away) that your lights or water are turned off, and if not, to turn them off. And, of course, you'll have better-quality reception in all these than you now have from broadcasts.

The whole system would be connected to a computer, which any subscriber could query for information. It is technically possible for each of us to have a complete computer terminal, with the whole Telex-type keyboard, and display tube, but it would be expensive. Peter Goldmark suggests a simple and much cheaper substitute, a sort of "twenty questions" gadget, with just a few buttons, perhaps on the TV set. It would be, he says, like "choosing from a menu. With each incoming frame the user is asked to choose one of several alternatives (up to ten) to define more precisely the information he wants. For example, if he were seeking travel information, he would with the first frame indicate whether he wanted to go by airplane, train, bus, or taxicab. The second frame (if he chose, say, air travel) would enable him to specify what airport he would use. The process would continue until the user had before him on his television screen the schedule of all airline flights of interest." He could press his "frame-grabber" at any stage and have all the information printed, in his hand, within perhaps a minute or two after pushing the first button.[2]

Dr. Goldmark goes further (still keeping well within our present technology) and suggests three kinds of cable (or other broad-band) networks, the first similar to the one just described, and organized into neighborhood subcenters of perhaps 3,000 to 15,000 homes, with local services and information.

The second would be another broad-band "pipe" carrying "the equivalent of 30 television channels in both directions. It would interconnect the major public institutions of the city, such as health, education, or emergency services."

As an example of what this could accomplish, the Massachusetts General Hospital in Boston is now connected by two-way television link with a Veterans Administration Hospital in Bedford, seventeen miles away. Specialists in Boston can examine patients in Bedford, read electrocardiograms, examine X rays, and so on, and give immediate advice. In the future, vast remote areas like parts of Alaska, northern Canada, Brazil, Africa, or the Australian outback could all be linked by broad-band communications and satellite with medical centers, giving advice to local doctors or even to nurses and partially qualified medical assistants. No new technology is needed, just money, work, and the cutting of miles of red tape.

The third network would represent what Dr. Goldmark calls the city's "sensory nerves," sending information to administrative centers on weather, pollution, traffic, the location of ambulances or fire engines or other emergency vehicles, and so on. Of course, most of this is now done to some extent by telephone, but the cable would expand the services greatly.

But possibly the most valuable use of the broad-band system, supplemented probably by domestic satellite, would be in education. This is such a big subject it will need a chapter of its own.

If all these wonders are possible now, why can't we have them? In a very good and often angry book Brenda Maddox explains why we can't, in convincing detail. Every legislator, and, in fact, every concerned citizen, should read it.[3]

Incredible as it sounds cable TV has been for all practical purposes excluded from almost every major city in the United States.

"There has been," says Mrs. Maddox, "a greater

choice of television in northern Vermont or Montana than there is in Boston and Pittsburgh. . . . The tough restrictions of the FCC have kept cable television from selling its most desirable product—out of town television programs—in the 100 biggest television markets. . . . The great information medium of tomorrow, in other words, has been excluded from cities larger than Augusta, Maine."[4]

The villain, of course, as Mrs. Maddox makes clear, is not just the FCC, but also all those people who are afraid that cable TV will make them lose money— especially the commercial television broadcasters. They're afraid it will reduce their audiences, and they've fought it bitterly.

In fact, the FCC became one of the villains by trying, earlier, to be a hero. When our UHF television was developed, it meant there could be more television channels than with the old longer wavelengths. The well-meaning but slightly addled FCC rushed in to encourage local people to set up their own UHF television stations, as an addition to the standard network fare.

Doesn't that sound reasonable, and idealistic, and totally good? But as any broadcaster could have told them, very few local groups can afford to do the kind of programming on a full-time basis that even their neighbors would want to watch. They could give local services and information, but the entertainment often rotted down to ancient movies. Many of the UHF stations went bankrupt, and the FCC, feeling guilty for encouraging them, tried to help. Part of that help was to fight cable TV, which they felt might be the final straw to break UHF's back.

The commercial networks were happy to join the FCC in jumping on cable TV, and the whole battle was almost like a gang war, with the cables coming out last. Their biggest stronghold is New York City, and that's largely because of all the tall buildings. In many parts of New York you can't get a decent picture without a cable. But even in New York programs produced in another city—even nearby Philadelphia or Boston—cannot be brought in by cable.

The other major possibility is the communications satellite, and it is being hog-tied almost as efficiently as cable TV.

There are really two uses of a communications satellite, and at the moment we're concentrating on just one—as a substitute for ocean cables. As Hiroshi Inose, a Japanese professor of electrical engineering, points out,[5] satellites can serve in parallel with ocean cables; a cable system can cost $150 million, is very reliable, and should work for longer than twenty years. A satellite, like *Intelsat IV*, orbits every twenty-four hours, 22,300 miles high, and seems to stay in the same position. It costs about $30 million for construction and launching and has an estimated life of seven years. We can lay any number of cables, but satellites, if orbiting too close together, can interfere with one another. So there's really nothing new about this use of a satellite; it's a sort of instant-cable and works very well.

The whole earth can now be reached by the Intelsat satellites. According to my information from Comsat Laboratories, four of the big new *Intelsat IV*'s, weighing over sixteen hundred pounds each, are in position over the Atlantic, Pacific, and Indian oceans, each capable of handling twelve television channels or more than three thousand telephone calls at once. There are also several of the smaller No. III's in orbit. All of them are used primarily for telephone service and occasional television relays. And there is no question that larger and more efficient ones will be developed.

However, it's the second use of satellites that should be far more important in the future, because it's something that perhaps *only* a satellite can do—to spread information to every remote corner of the world. Used together with local cable systems, they could do almost anything we can imagine.

At the moment, the Intelsats send only to the big-dish antennae at the Intelsat ground stations, but new transmitters already developed will enable them to send to much smaller installations and eventually to home antennae. For example, in the educational television system now being planned for India (more about this later) villages will be able to build their own antennae out of chicken wire for as little as twenty-five dollars—and receive the signal coming from 22,300 miles away!

Satellites now orbit directly above oceans to connect continents, but the great satellites of the future will hover above continents to connect people.

Probably the first plan to do this was prepared by an American, Fred Friendly, for the Ford Foundation, back in 1966. He said there should be a domestic satellite, and it should be owned by the public. (In fact, it is amazing that *all* satellites are not at least 90 percent owned by the public, because it was the public, through taxes, who paid almost all the cost of development, as part of the multibillion-dollar space program. The greatest cost, of course, was the development of the rockets to put them up there.) This publicly owned satellite, Friendly suggested, could transmit the commercial television programs—could do it for less than they were paying for wire transmission—and make enough money to pay for educational and other non-commercial programming, which it could then broadcast to local town antennae and rebroadcast to the whole country, free.

It was too good to be true, or to be allowed. One problem was that the FCC was already considering proposals by the American Broadcasting Company to put up its own satellite. Brenda Maddox, who does a superb documentation of the whole satellite-throttling tragedy, says, "The practical effect of the Ford plan, in fact, was to paralyze the FCC by making the issue seem even more complicated than it had originally."[6]

The upshot of all this is that the United States has never had a domestic satellite, though at least two are now flying for other countries and broadcasting. On October 14, 1972, the Russians put up their *Molniya 1*, a domestic satellite for their own people, which followed by about two weeks *Molniya II*, intended for world communications.[7] And on November 9 NASA launched *ANIK-1* for Canada, capable of broadcasting ten channels of television, in both French and English, to all of Canada, including the vast and previously unreachable northern country. It will also make telephone communications possible from the U.S. border to the Arctic circle.

So we've done it for Canada—for Canadian Telesat, which is both a private and a public corporation—though there's still too much corporate and bureaucratic red tape to let us do it for ourselves. However, in June 1972, the FCC did at last vote to allow "qualified applicants" to provide domestic satellite service for TV, telephone, telegraph, and computer data service.[8]

And NASA, to its credit, is putting up a domestic satellite for India, too. This could be the most amazing use of educational television in history. The Indians plan eventually to broadcast to half a million villages, to teach people to read and write, how to use birth control, and how to farm with modern methods. Brazil, too, is planning such a system to serve her enormous inland and jungle areas. It is these formerly unreachable places that satellites serve best.

We'll put them up for others, as we should, but our own people may be last. "After all, old boy, you can't step on all those toes, can you? Think what it would do to the ratings!"

American noncommercial television and educational channels will continue to limp along, begging for handouts, scrimping on programming, the ragged urchin of the world's richest country. There is no need to shackle commercial TV. The two can coexist, as they do peacefully in England or even as they do in most European countries where television is publicly run, but where paid commercial advertisements are inserted, usually in bunches, but never in the middle of a film, a play, or a concert. This is something that happens only to Americans.

Or, as a BBC viewer said to me after a visit to America, "Occasionally the advertising is interrupted by entertainment."

If we're going to get a future with really intelligent or informative television fare, and material for minority groups of all kinds, if we want something beyond the bland pudding we're getting now, then we're going to have to act like the citizens of a democracy and elect people who will make the laws to make it possible.

Our constitutional right of freedom of speech must, in the future, include the right of the free speech to reach us. At the moment we're like a man dropped to the bottom of a well and told that he may speak freely about anything.

Whatever new means of communication we develop —television, facsimile, holography, or anything else— must, like book publishing today, be open to all comers, to all intellectual ranges, and to all opinions. Because these media are expensive to use, it is going to take a lot of figuring, but it is going to have to be done. We cannot let new technologies be stopped because they may compete with some older system. Technically, we can now do almost anything—but we must be allowed to do it.

11

THE ELECTRICAL PARADISE

*How to make your home
the center of the world*

Let's suppose, then, that we've succeeded democrati-
cally and elected brave, clean young men as legislators,
who have cut through all the red tape and skulduggery
of bumbling bureaucrats and greedy vested interests,
and have finally given the air and the sky and the cables
to the people.

Then let's assume that we'll have some of the other
wonders that are already invented. The most obvious
are video cassettes, which Brenda Maddox dismisses
with an airy wave of the hand as "the television set's
phonograph records." That they are, to be sure, but
they have the great advantage that they are immune to
the strange conniptions of the FCC and the broadcasters. They can come striding right into your home, and
none of these characters can lay a hand on them.

The main reason everyone doesn't have them now is

that there have been so many different noncompatible systems; i.e., all the tapes won't play on all the machines. Some have optical "tape"—actually like movie film—and one was based on holography (of which more later). This is still a problem, but the most expensive part of making a cassette is obviously the production of the show or program. Once produced, it can be transferred to most systems (though not, of course, to holography).

Cassettes and their recorders and playback machines are in many thousands of homes now, and "cassette clauses" are written into every television, film, and book contract. Nobody wants to lose his cassette rights because everyone feels that eventually cassettes will inherit the world.

In the future major productions will be undertaken primarily for cassettes. They can be, and certainly will be, produced like books, for any minority taste, from children's programs to commercial comedies to eroticism and all the way to the most avant-garde and intellectual films and filmed plays. Like books and films, they don't require instant success; they can pay off their cost of production over years of sales and library rentals. There will certainly be big cassette rental libraries and probably weekly or monthly subscriptions.

Cassettes will go hand in hand with broad-band communication, like cable TV, if we ever get it, not only as broadcast material but as a way of recording anything transmitted that we want to keep.

The next real wonder that may replace, or at least

supplement, the television tube is motion-holography. Dennis Gabor won a Nobel Prize for inventing this ingenious method of photographing in the round, using laser beams, making a film that looks like a child's finger painting of whorls within whorls, which is projected wondrously and three-dimensionally into space —say, into the middle of your living room. Unlike those binocular "3-D" movies, this is a true image in depth—you can see different facets of it from different angles.

Holography was developed first in still-picture form, and even with this we could, for example, bring the entire New York Auto Show to a cabin in Montana, projecting one full-sized car at a time. Or you could have Michelangelo's *David* (or any other sculpture) in your living room, changing at the press of a button to *King Kong*, Brigitte Bardot, or the sarcophagus of King Tut.

Eventually, holography will be perfected in motion and sound (it's already in color) and broadcast, or broad-banded, cassetted, or sent by satellite. Nureyev could dance on your dining room table if you wanted him to (without getting his feet in the gravy)—and life size! Want your own dancing girl? Buy the cassette! The educational possibilities are endless, and the erotic possibilities enough to blow the mind.

Perhaps the ultimate communication will be directly into your brain. One day it will be possible to become a part of your computer, or have it become a part of you. Your brain, which is really a bioelectronic instrument, will be linked to a computer. No need to type out your requirements or even to speak them to the computer (this is in its early stages of development now)—just *think!*" "I wonder how to say that in Chinese," you think, and the computer will pop it into your head.

This mind-computer link is called symbiosis, and the Rand Corporation predicts it will happen by the end of the century. And if you have a computer into which virtually all knowledge has been stored—including the five hundred scientific papers that were put into it last Tuesday—then you'll know it all, too!

Now, this is bound to have some effect on your personality:

"Well, yes, Harry's all right when he's hooked up to his 3700-2B, but alone he's impossible."

Or, on the contrary:

"Mary's quite charming alone. Just make sure you unplug her from her Honeywell."

Needless to say, this is bound to have a really revolutionary effect on art, if we can still call it that. As everyone knows, computers are even now composing music and doing a bit of writing. With symbiosis, perhaps the novelist will only have to *think* of a scene and characters, and the computer will have the whole thing in typescript ninety seconds later. Computer tubes have, for years, been doing finished architectural drawings and industrial designs, based on rough light-pen sketches. The symbiotic computer should be able to illustrate, in full color, the barest flicker of a mental image.

The depth and complexity of symbiotic art may be far beyond the unassisted critic, and this will lead to the computer-assisted literary, art, or music critic, the only one able to demolish the work of the other symbiotic collaborators.

And nothing is surer than this: There will be other, unimaginable technological wonders to come. In fact, I invented (or at least projected) a rather ultimate one myself, in a science fiction novel called *The Big Ball of Wax*, years ago. Perhaps some of you will be able to fill in the technical details; if so, I'll be glad to share the profits. I called it XP, for "experience." Since nerve impulses are basically electrical, we simply need to find a way to tap them. You can tap a telephone wire without touching it, by induction. Once you have recorded the nerve impulses on magnetic tape, you can then play them, also by induction, directly into the brain, with a playback machine that looks like a helmet. All the sensory impulses, sight, sound, smell, feeling, and taste, are duplicated, so that you're not watching, you're *doing*— eating a twenty-course dinner (for less cost in electricity than frying an egg), doing a hundred-meter ski jump, making love to a dozen of the most beautiful women (or the handsomest, sexiest men) in one evening—and it's better than the real thing if you turn the volume up double or triple. Things like that.

Neurologists tell me that XP will take a bit of doing, but it's no more unthinkable than men on the moon were thirty years ago.

Suppose, then, that XP will take awhile, but the others all come true. What will happen then? Instant paradise? Perhaps, if we're very careful, but the odds are against it. Mead's Law of Electrical Entertainment is: Content normally moves in inverse ratio to technology —or, the pictures keep gettin' better, and the plays keep gettin' worse.

For example, in the early 1950s we had only black and white television, and some of the white was "snow." But the great television playhouses were going strong. Remember *Studio One* and some of the early TV plays of Paddy Chayevsky and Rod Serling? Then along came Joe McCarthy and pressure groups, and pretty soon sponsors were terrified to say anything that might offend anybody anywhere. A lot of the good people just left television.

And so now we have lovely color (though nothing like as lovely as European color)—and the plays? The corners have to be cut off everything. That always leaves a blob shape, the shape of something that can go in all directions at once. Art of any kind that tries to mean all things to all men usually winds up meaning nothing to anyone.

It doesn't have to be that way. Try to buck the trend. If you don't want to go to the future of the idiot children, you'll have to push hard. Otherwise the end result may be shining, impeccable reality, sitting on your carpet and blubbering its three-dimensional lips.

Some experts say that international communications —such as television beamed by satellite to many countries—can be a great unifying force, can help to join together the peoples of the world. Hopefully, yes. But as Brenda Maddox points out, the danger is that they will appeal to the lowest common denominator because "every statement is overexplained, the comedy is slapstick, the smiles too broad, the whole program having been designed to give a minimum of offense to a wider than usual number of people."[1] I've watched the programs of Eurovision, the European television network, and I agree. The abominable yahoos of television can be even worse, in five languages.

In the "software" of electrical wonders—the thinking part—we shall have to do the hardest work of all.

The Electronic Household

No work of this kind is complete without a visit to the home of the future, where everything is unbearably miraculous. Shall we drop in on the exurban Joneses just a few years from now?

Their house is far from the city where Mr. Jones's computer is located. (They've been talking about an air-cushion monorail with a linear electric motor that will go 275 miles an hour, but actually they're still using that commuter train with the 1937 cars and the torn cushions.)

Jones goes into the city only every week or two. When we join them, he is sitting in his soundproof office-den—every man has one—and attending a business meeting, even though he is entirely alone. He is dressed in business clothes, but only above the waist. Below the tabletop he has on tennis shoes and shorts, unseen by the phonavision. His background is carefully arranged, including a bookshelf full of beautifully bound volumes that Jones has always been intending to read. The opposite wall is a mess; the sweaty tennis shirt is hanging on a hook, beside a water ski that he has been repairing. The phonavee, of course, doesn't look in that direction.

Jones works for a firm of plumbing contractors. A facsimile of their latest advertisement has just slid out of the fax machine, on top of a piece of paper that slid out five minutes before (the most recent price list on the super-washbowl series, up 3 percent from last month). He can see in his phonavee that B.J., his group supervisor, has the ad in his hand. The red light on the phonavee goes on, and Jones knows he's on camera.

"Let me have your thoughts on it, Jonesy," says B.J.

Jones clears his throat and says, "I think it's a nice job, B.J.—but if you don't mind, I'd like to tee off a bit on this blurb from the housewife."

The basic ways of succeeding at meetings haven't changed. The man who doesn't really like what they're talking about still looks better than the man who does.

It should be added that Jones's office-den also includes a complete computer terminal, with a typewriter keyboard and display tube. He *has* to have one. It's a status symbol and is supplied by his company. Not to have one is to seem illiterate. Actually, Jones is terrified of it, uses it mainly just for information and to work out his income tax figures. He still pecks at the keyboard with two fingers.

In the next room (unheard by Jonesy) his wife is startled by their little daughter, who bursts in, shouting, "I wanna dog, Mommy!"

"Quiet, dear, Mommy's shopping."

She is, too. She's looking at the latest dresses at Saks Fifth Avenue, on television, on a wall-sized screen. As the models go by, she presses a button.

"May I help you, Modom?" says a voice.

"How much is that red off-the-shoulder number?"

"Three-five, Modom," says the voice, meaning $3,500. "It's a special today."

"That's very reasonable," Mrs. J. says. "Can you fit me?" She stands in front of the metric scale on the wall, done sort of like graph paper, but *nice* graph paper. It has her computer number on it, too.

"I've got a fax of it now, Modom. It would look *lovely* on you, and I'm sure we can do something clever about the waistline."

"Your computer has all the exact dimensions."

"Yes, Modom, you'll have it tomorrow."

"Thank you," she says, and turns off the wall.

"I wanna dog, Mommy."

"Well, turn it on, dear."

"I got it on, it's a alligator now."

Mrs. J. opens the door wider and can see there is, indeed, an alligator waddling around on the nursery floor. At that moment it snaps off, and a holographic armadillo, life size, is turning around in circles.

"Just wait, dear," says Mrs. J. "They always end up with the doggies."

An alarm bell rings, and Mrs. J. plunges into her TV chair and snaps on the wall. A floor-to-ceiling-size man's face, oozing charm (it was tested against 678 other charm-oozing faces) with a voice calculated to drive women mad (it was tested against 854 other voices) says, "Hello, hello, everyone! It's time for the Money-O! Press the old button-O and let us know you're here-io! We're giving away another million buck-ios today—and here we go-io!"

Mrs. J. trembles with excitement, because the Money-O does really give away a million dollars a day —and that's a lot of money, as much as a good secretary can earn in several months. Pricewise, the Money-O program is an advertising bargain, because some 54 million people watch and button it every day, so it's less than two cents a guaranteed, buttoned viewer.

Mrs. J. presses a series of "Who Are Ya?" buttons, which establish her precisely, marketwise, as a Class B housewife, with two children, preteen and teen-age, her car and house category, and her sales-psych susceptibility rating (worked out for everyone by sales-psychologists: "Are you more influenced by hard sell or soft sell? Jingle-prone? Your sex-din rating, or cuddle-quotient, and so on.). All admen had known for years that most advertising—those seven-hundred-odd messages that battered everyone every day—was wasted, walloping ten-year-olds with copy for false-teeth stickum and retirement bungalows, fifty-year-old maidens with maternity dresses and jockey briefs, truck drivers with panty-girdles, and so on. The Money-O never wastes a word. Once locked in, pressing her buttons every thirty seconds in reply to questions, Mrs. Jones is supplied with a series of commercials chosen just for her category. And they *know* she's listening—

"Just keep pushin' those old button-O's, friend-ios, and you'll be eligible for the Money-O. Every day *somebody* wins!"

So Mrs. Jones sits there, being filled with uncontrollable desire and ordering things on the spot by pressing order buttons.

Actually on this day she wins nothing but a small hundred-dollar tube of toothpaste, and she feels a bit cheated.

None of this, however, is heard by Junior, who is in his room attending a lecture at the Open University, being given at Cambridge, in England. It's getting so the family can't understand a word he says.

A Footnote on Meetings

Many business meetings in the future may be like the one we've just attended, and those of you who really want to succeed in the coming electronic paradise will have to work out new ways to cope with the phonavee meeting.

We all know that it isn't what is actually *said* at a business meeting that means anything, it is what is left unsaid—the slight lifting of an eyebrow, eyeballs rolled almost imperceptibly heavenward, a shrug, or even a doodle (scrawled with apparent unconcern on a note pad)—that tells your troops when to attack, retreat, or stage a flanking maneuver. New methods will have to be found when everyone is in a different room, or even in different cities, to give important signals.

The fellow who learns how to get one up on this kind of meeting will rule the business world of tomorrow. Find your own ways; perhaps you'll gain some nourishment in these areas:

1. *The premeeting meeting,* held by phonavee with your own troops, to brief them on general strategy.

2. *A clever use of facsimile memos.* No one, of course, reads long memos, so instructions to your troops can be inserted, say, in the seventeenth subpoint of Proposal III or any other prearranged position that is beyond the scope of the casual reader.

And remember, the age-old principle will not change: The purpose of a meeting, electronic or otherwise, is to make you look good in it, to propel you ever upward.

A Note about Advertising

Advertising has trained itself to be the handmaiden of industry, and in the future this will be even more so. As admen make ever-increasing use of psychology and market research, they will become more and more effective, to the point of being virtually irresistible.

This can, of course, be an almost omnipotent force

for good—that is, if it is used for good. Admen, like mules, will go where they are prodded to go. Given the proper incentive (i.e., money) and pointed in the right direction, they are quite capable of saving the world. Point them, and pay them, and they will amaze us all.

Let's suppose, for example, that worse comes to worst. We have failed in our efforts to stem the tide. The hobgoblins of the Club of Rome and its M.I.T. computers are swarming after us, making dread electronic queeps. All the lines on the graphs are going down, and we're on one of them.

We're beginning just slightly to gasp for air, to edge away from the rising, bubbling sewage, to be tightly pressed by the exploding population, and to look, in vain, for our irreplaceable resources. There's no point in selling a man air conditioning if there's no air to condition (and no electricity to condition it with) or persuading him to buy a gold-plated 2,000-horsepower Cadillac if there's no gas to go in it and no place to drive except through rusting piles of obsolete 1,800-horsepower gold-plated Cadillacs.

Is everything lost? Not at all. It is the time to call in the admen. They have been told to make us want the things we don't need. Tell them to turn around the other way. We all know about negative income tax. Tell them to begin negative, or reverse, advertising. And give them 15 percent of everything.

"How much is everything?" they will say.

"We don't know, but it is better than fifteen percent of nothing."

They will go off into brainstorm sessions—or conferences in which everyone talks at once and throws ideas into the air—being careful not to throw any really good ones, but to save those for a memo later. An idea that doesn't have your name on it is like a day without sunshine.

They will come up with wondrous things. For example, a junior copywriter may think he has discovered a new principle: "Why not," he would write in a memo, "make them want only things that are old? The antique business is based on this principle." And that is so.

The Antique Syndrome Can Save the World

"To be a genuine antique," they say now, "it must be at least one hundred years old!" The idea is sound, but one hundred years is too long. Shift it to—say—thirty?

Is it full of wormholes? So much the better. It's genuine! Is it all worn out? Correction: The word is "patina"—that lovely, smooth, threadbare feeling.

Do you know that a 1927 Rolls-Royce recently sold for $125,000? That an auction was held at the 1973 auto show in Geneva, and a 1908 Benz, with a performance about equal to that of a 1923 Essex, sold for 260,000 Swiss francs, which is around $80,000? Or that Greta Garbo's old Duesenberg brought $95,000? Priced any Model-A Fords lately?

The new, future commercials will have people saying, "Oh, you have a *modern* car!" with just a trace of pity and condescension.

"You mean," the man in the dramatization says, "it's a genuine 1970 Maverick—not a copy?"

"No, I've had it authenticated! The real thing, engine numbers and all! Look at that rust! Converted to hydrogen, of course, but the same coachwork! Still has the Tiger in the Tank sticker on it!"

"I'll give you seven million for it!"

It will become an in-thing to decorate your walls with flattened tin cans or to construct mosaics out of broken Coke bottles. And all of it, of course, will save the world.

The admen will never go backward, they will go forward, or at you, and it will be for your own good.

Future Super-Games

Once it becomes anti-eco to ride around and burn up resources, people will find other, more subtle ways of bashing into each other. One way will be fascinating new variations of the future super-games, or we might call them relevance games.

Some of these are played with computers, and this gives you that sense of proprietary power that you used to have when you bore down on your fellowman in that 600-horsepower Grand Prix Mach 2 GT Blunder-Bus. Sitting smugly at the keyboard of your IBM-8400, you can rev up your memory cores and bellow a challenge to your neighbor, armed to the teeth with his Honeywell Super-Bull.

These games are an outgrowth of the earlier war games (or peace games if you prefer) as played by the think-tank boys at the Rand Corporation, or Herman Kahn at the Hudson Institute, making computer models of nuclear warfare and writing scenarios about the unthinkable.

The forerunners of these computerized fencing matches of the future are being played now. One of them, described in the most incomprehensible detail in a current IBM research and development report, is called An Interactive Computer-Based Game for Decision-Making in Ecology, and I call it the Garbage Game. The players, safely strapped in at their computer controls, fingers splayed out offensively on their keyboards, try to find the best way to route a garbage pickup truck. Or, to put it in IBM-ese, "A scenario is written that involves players in routing problems. . . . Each player at a terminal has the impression that he has his own computer at all times. . . ."

It is, of course, a farsighted way to sell computers, for the leisure trade.

I'd suggest to IBM, though, that they raise their sights from garbage to something sexier, like money, to make a kind of super Monopoly. For example, you and your future neighbor might cross swords (i.e., computers) in a stock market game:

"George and Harry are at it again with their computers!"

"The Garbage Game?"

"The market, dear. The game is to figure out which stock will go higher."

"How do they keep score?"

"With money, dear. Actually, Harry is ahead. He's made seven hundred and ninety-four thousand dollars more than George. It's a lovely game. I've bought two mink coats and a weekend cottage since they started."

You will need more than sweat socks and a squash racket but if you play it properly, the equipment will pay for itself.

12

HOW TO FILL YOUR HEAD
WITH THE FUTURE

Will electric education save the world
or blow your mind?

Do you consider yourself educated? Just because you have that degree? Even *you*, with the Ph.D.? What does being "educated" mean today? What is the best education to give your child as a preparation for the future? In fact, is it possible to prepare for this future at all?

Which of the following statements is true?

"Dear boy, it is impossible to be educated today, and utterly unthinkable in the future!"

"Relax, man, relax! What's education? Facts, right? In the future, man, nobody will have to know any facts at all!"

"The university is out of date. The old ways can't cope with the knowledge explosion! Use electronics— or quit!"

"I can *prove* to you that educational television is almost worthless!"

Who's right? Well, there are ample facts to back up each one of those statements.

Just a century ago it was possible for a truly well-educated man to know almost all the important knowledge accumulated by mankind. If that means being "educated," it is absolutely impossible for any human to be educated today. Human knowledge is expanding so rapidly that no one can catch up with it.

If you were the world's best student, took a four-year university course, and if you could even theoretically learn "everything"—then the day you finished you would have to begin again, because human knowledge would have doubled during the four years. Or, as Robert Hilliard, an education specialist for the Federal Communications Commission, put it: "By the time the child born today graduates from college, the amount of knowledge will be four times as great. By the time the same child is 50 years old, it will be 32 times as great, and 97% of everything known in the world will have been learned since he was born."[1]

The memorizing of reams of facts won't be necessary; they'll be quickly available in computers, as we've seen, but you will have to know what you want. Otherwise you'll be like a child standing in the middle of the New York Public Library. He has learned to read, and he could within an hour or so find almost any known fact—but he doesn't even know what it is he wants to know.

Future man will need great knowledge if only to know what to ask, if only to have the tools and building blocks of thought. To think without knowledge is like painting without paint.

If we're going to cope with the future at all, we shall certainly have to reorganize and vastly improve both our methods of education and the choice of things that we teach.

Most of our education is based on the past and taught by ancient and obsolete methods. The main purpose of much of it simply seems to be to earn "credits," based on examinations, which attempt to prove that a student has succeeded in memorizing a series of facts, many of which are no longer relevant to anything he'll ever experience in life.

For example, it is possible for a student in England to graduate from a university (say, Oxford or Cambridge) never having come in contact with anything (since the age of about sixteen) written since the year A.D. 400! (It is also possible, if he's in the Cambridge molecular biology laboratory, to be staring right into the eyes of the future.)

It's possible for a student in the ghetto area of Detroit to be automatically promoted to high school level without being able to read or write.

In many of the developing countries illiteracy is so high, and all forms of advanced education so scarce, that the old-fashioned methods of teaching may never catch up. Without new methods all these people may simply be left behind by the exploding growth of new knowledge.

What to teach could fill volumes. We'll consider

mainly *how* to teach. We have to use many new ways, and we have already experimented with some fascinating ones. Are they going to be good enough?

How to Teach with Electricity

Part of the new education will certainly use broadcasting and new electronic audiovisual devices and techniques. However, if we just lie back and say, "The gimmicks will do it!"—then we're bound to fail.

It is like saying: "What is teaching? Talking and writing on the blackboard, isn't it?" Anyone can prove that inspired teaching has been done this way, and also abominably bad teaching.

The electronic devices can, for one thing, take brilliant teaching and multiply it a million times. They can do the same for bad teaching. And if relied upon entirely, to the extent that live teaching is eliminated, they could be disastrous.

Brenda Maddox says, "The world is littered with failed educational television projects,"[2] and so it is. Developing nations have a kind of pathetic hope that the wonder gimmick of the satellite, broadcasting down to everyone, will solve everything. The more sophisticated countries know that the gadgets alone are not enough, and they've already seen them fail.

Mrs. Maddox cites the Midwest Airborne Television Experiment. Instead of spending some $30 million to put up a satellite, the Ford Foundation simulated it by having an airplane fly over Illinois all day, beaming down educational television programs to schools. But the programs weren't yet properly prepared or conceived, and the teachers (the ones on the ground) weren't adequately informed or sufficiently persuaded to cooperate—and most of them didn't even turn on the sets. The project was a failure.

The British, probably the most experienced users of educational broadcasting, are also wary of half-baked television teaching systems in developing countries. Their Centre for Educational Television Overseas reported in 1969 that "all too frequently, programs are produced which meet no defined need and which are not educationally valid. This devalues the service, disappoints the teachers in the classroom and the service eventually falls into disuse."[3]

But educational television has worked already. In American Samoa, beginning in 1963, it replaced the entire educational system, the old textbooks, and most of the classroom teachers. Trained television teaching teams came from the United States, and education was considerably improved, though at a high cost. With television teaching, however, the smaller the number of students involved, the greater the cost per student. As the numbers vastly increase, costs per student can go down spectacularly.[4]

The French succeeded amazingly well in Niger, where French is the official language but where many of the young black children hadn't ever heard it spoken. After a year of television instruction, with almost no live teachers at all, 90 percent of the one thousand test pupils read French better than the national average.[5] This seems to prove that languages can be taught by television alone.

I have no doubt that television, properly used, could end illiteracy throughout the world. In fact, used intelligently, it could bring education of almost any level almost anywhere. The key words are "properly used."

I think of two specific examples, one at the lowest primary level and one at a much higher level. The first, *Sesame Street*, is known to every American. And now, through foreign broadcasts in English, and even many dubbed in foreign languages, it is moving around the world. *Sesame Street* is designed for preschool children, to entertain them and to give them a kind of head start in learning to read, to do a bit of arithmetic, and even learn some basic social attitudes, like racial tolerance.

It uses just about any device that will fascinate children: live action with actors, and also with huge people-filled puppets and with small puppets, with animation, singing, dancing, games—almost anything at all—and done in almost whooping good humor and usually broken down into very short bits, lasting sometimes less than a minute, because the attention span of young children is short. Mrs. Maddox quotes the result:

> The Educational Testing Service of Princeton found that it imparted the ability to recognize the letters of the alphabet, the numbers from one to ten, and certain basic concepts such as the similarity and dissimilarity of objects. Better still, the ETS found that the program

was not (as its critics charged) reaching only middle-class children whose mothers were keen that they watch it but also children from much poorer homes, who were presumably less supervised. The results showed that the children from slum homes who watch *Sesame Street* frequently learned more than middle-class children who watched it infrequently. The conclusion was "that such television programs can reduce the distinct educational gap that usually separates advantaged and disadvantaged children even by the time they enter first grade (at the age of six)."[6]

I'll argue with Mrs. Maddox about one thing only. She felt it was very expensive, doing its job only "at a price." The price? Eight million dollars for the first twenty-six weeks, one hour a day, five days a week. During its first season *Sesame Street* had an audience of 7 million children. (It's bigger now.) That is about *one* dollar per child for six months—or about four cents per child per week, for five hours of instruction! Would you pay a penny a day to have your preschool children taught, say, French or German? It should be quite possible to do this using the *Sesame Street* methods.

But the cost isn't even *that* much. The audience keeps growing up, and away, and nearly all the material can be used again and again. I'd say it's one of the biggest teaching bargains in history.

Does television teaching have to be on a kindergarten level? It does not. I was convinced years ago that television could teach on almost any level, because I lived for some years in England and watched BBC programs on really mind-shattering subjects. One of these was a series on the theory of relativity, which made it clearer to me than any other medium had ever been able to do before.

The best example, though, was an incredible series of programs given late at night on molecular biology by John Kendrew, a biochemist and Nobel Prize winner. Was it possible to explain to lay minds the difficult concepts of the DNA molecule? Kendrew himself had made some of the key discoveries in this field. He's a witty man and a good teacher. He didn't merely talk to us; he let us look through microscopes at living cells, showed us how we could see things much smaller than the wavelength of light by X-ray crystallography, making crystals of molecules and using them as a lens for X rays, projecting pictures on a screen. He didn't just *tell* us about it; we watched the whole process of discovery, close up, as though Kendrew were sitting across the table from us. He led us into crystalline structures. He'd tell the camera, "Come right in here on the angle of this pencil," and we'd see a whole screen full of tiny structures, from an inch away.

No university lecture I ever attended could approach it, and couldn't even if Kendrew himself were in the lecture theater, because he could bring us right up to his very fingertips. It was more exciting than a detective film. The ideas were complex almost beyond description (by words alone), yet made so clear that any junior high school student could have followed them easily.

This kind of treatment could—with great artistry and intelligence—be given to every facet of knowledge. It means that an inspired teacher like Kendrew can be multiplied a millionfold, and brought into every school, or every home, of the English-speaking world, and even dubbed into other languages. It doesn't replace live teachers in the classroom. John Kendrew, on a cassette, can't answer their questions. But it can light up live teachers, too, with the excitement and fascination of knowledge.

What Makes a Good Educational Program?

On the basis of these programs, and of many years of work with broadcasting audiences, I'd say there are a number of minimum essentials for any educational broadcasting material, in addition to its factual content:

1. *It must be fascinating* so that an audience, which can always tune out without embarrassment (like the embarrassment of walking out of a classroom when the going gets dull), will continue to watch it with interest, and even with pleasure. This means that it must be done with a degree of *genius*. Both the above examples were done with genius. And for this, there are plenty of geniuses to go around, because one really brilliant teacher can reach millions of people. (It is almost certain that in the future there will be great "star" teachers, known throughout the world.)

Also it means, genius or no, that you must *test* it on live people before you send it out, and ruthlessly throw out whatever does *not* fascinate people. There is no way for a forty-two-year-old educational programmer (even a genius) to know exactly what fascinates a four-year-old child, except to sit a group of four-year-olds down in front of a tube and watch them. You can tell right away. They do this on *Sesame Street*. On a closed circuit (that is, inside your studio, with the set connected by a wire to the camera, not broadcast) you can pipe in any material, either live or on film or tape. The parts that don't fascinate, no matter how much you love them, you cut. (They do this, too, on *Sesame Street*.)

It is true, of course, that after you have tested a few hundred things, you will know a great deal more about just what does fascinate people, and your batting average will improve. This should not, however, prevent you from trying new things about which you're not yet sure.

2. *It must be intelligible.* You can fascinate with tricks, but your message—the subject or material you're trying to teach—can go over their heads. You will have to test this, too. Ask questions of your studio audience, or even give them tests. Are they getting it?

3. *It cannot be condescending.* If you make an audience of any level think you are talking down to them, you have lost them. If children feel you are patting them on the head, they will turn you off.

4. *It must be get-at-able,* reachable, askable, even look-up-able. This may be a weakness of *Sesame Street,*

but at that age level this could be overlooked. At any more complex level, there must be some way for students to ask questions, to hear again something they missed, or be able to look up and learn complex material.

There are all kinds of ways to do this, but it must be done *some* way. The best way is to have an informed, live teacher there, or at least on hand after the lesson is over—one who knows the material and can answer questions that will be raised by the material. Some educational TV systems propose to have other, supplementary programs for the teachers. India, for example, with its satellite education program, plans to be training teachers simultaneously with special broadcasts for them.

Another way is to supply students with books or mimeographed material—formulas, dates, verb conjugations, and so on—to supplement the programs. The printed information might contain the entire lecture, plus other related material and reading lists. In a really well-organized future there would also be lists of cassettes of other related lectures.

Another way is to have all the lectures on cassettes. They could be sent in that form to the schools, or the schools could record them off the air. Tape-players can repeat any section of the material. For example, in language training it's helpful to go back again and again, repeating phrases.

Still another method is to have frame-grabbers on the television set, to take off any special material like maps, diagrams, and tables. And facsimile sets will be able to receive printed material of any kind. At first this equipment will be available only in the schools. Later it may be in every home.

An additional way to answer (or anticipate) most of the questions that occur to student audiences is to have the program screened before a live audience (or, better, several audiences) of students of the appropriate age level, and have them ask questions which are answered, live, by the lecturer himself if he is available or by a teacher familiar with the material. This question-and-answer session is broadcast after the lecture. If several student audiences are used, the material can be edited so that all the most useful questions and answers can be included.

5. *You must try, somehow, to "step up."* This is the most difficult concept of all, but unless you do it, you may fall into a rating trap, like so many commercial programs. This is especially true if you are concerned about the audience ratings of your program. You may become infected with the "poll mentality"—the dread disease that has almost destroyed American television. In your attempt to fascinate your audience, you may pander to them, you may find you are trying to appeal to the lowest common denominator, and your broadcasts will tend to become less and less intelligent. If you step up *too* much, if you become too advanced or difficult, you will lose them. But if you are careful and step up a very little bit at a time, you will bring them up with you—and that is really the object of the game.

Educational electronics, used this way, can work wonders, and perhaps even more wonders in the developing countries than in those that already have much more complete educational systems.

The British Open University

The first university of the future has already opened and is, today, teaching thousands of students. It is the most thorough experiment yet carried out in electronics-aided education, and it is operating in Great Britain, which already has a highly developed conventional system of education.

The British Open University was planned to make it possible for everyone, even those who are working full-time, and those who have no secondary school credits or any official qualifications, to take university courses at home and to obtain degrees. The government decided in 1967 to start a "university of the air," and the first academic year began in January 1971. It now has six basic divisions: arts, mathematics, science, social sciences, technology, and educational studies.

The most important thing the government decided was that it isn't enough just to broadcast a lot of lectures. It is not called a "university of the air" at all now. It is, in fact (as I was told), a "multi-media" method of teaching, combining radio and television lectures with regular mailings (about once a week) of correspondence texts; regular personal meetings, every few weeks, with tutors; regular submission of written material, some graded by teachers and some by computers; large numbers of required books (many of them especially prepared for the Open University, and all, of course, on sale to the public as well); a week of summer school residence; and yearly examinations.

At the moment the Open University is concentrating on people who have missed university education and takes only students over twenty-one, though in 1974 it is starting a test group of five hundred under-twenty-ones.

It is possible for a person with a full-time job, taking a one-credit course every year, studying an average of ten to fifteen hours a week, to get a B.A. degree in six years. Or, on a more or less full-time basis, taking two courses a year, to get a degree in three years.

Part of the cost is paid by the government; the students pay from about $75 to $200 per course, or roughly $1,000 for a university education.

Suppose, for example, that you live anywhere in the British Isles, have a job, and want to begin your university education with the A100 course in the humanities, somewhat similar to a freshman general arts and literature course. It begins in January and will include thirty-four television lectures of twenty-five minutes each, on BBC-2. (Times given are the actual ones in the 1973 catalog schedule.)

The first broadcast is at 6:15 P.M. on Wednesdays, and if you miss that, it's repeated at 8:55 A.M. on Saturdays. There are also thirty-four radio broadcasts, the first each week at 11:35 A.M. on Saturdays, repeated at 6:45 P.M. on Fridays. If you miss any of these, you can arrange for replays at your local study center (which is probably at a nearby university or school; there are 280 such centers in Britain). Your own tutor, or personal teacher, will be there, too. He may be a local university tutor doing this part-time, or in a technical course he may be a professional chemist, engineer, or computer programmer.

You will probably confer with your tutor privately every few weeks. He's the one who will correct and grade your weekly written work and tests. In this particular course there are fifteen required books, all available in paperback. There will be other recommended reading, and you will receive weekly notes and assignments by mail.

If you were studying science, you would receive a home experiment kit, including more than one hundred chemicals, test tubes, a microscope especially developed for the Open University, and other materials. One course includes a binary computing device, a noise meter, and a tape recorder. These are all sent to you on loan; you pay a deposit. If you're studying computers, one of 160 computer terminals will be available to you.

In the summer you will spend a week in residence (usually at a university campus, during their vacation) for a summer school course. In October you will go to a study center for your written examination.

For students in remote areas—say, the Scottish Highlands or an island in the Hebrides—it is possible to manage it all by broadcast and by mail, coming to the study center only for the week of summer school and for the examination.

That's the theory of it all. How is it working?

I visited the modern, glassy building of the London Regional Headquarters on Grosvenor Street and talked to David Gellan, an administrative officer. He is an amiable, rather harried-looking young man who was wearing a leather coat and a pink shirt. Scrawled on his white-board in orange letters were the words "Remember, Rome wasn't built in a day, but Dresden was destroyed in a night." The impression is that it will take more than a day to build the Open University, but the foundations, at least, are surely being laid.

In the 1973 academic year there were about eight thousand registered paying students in the London region, and fewer than forty thousand nationally. I'd expected much larger numbers. Of course, many more people watch and hear the programs in a less disciplined manner. They're available free, naturally, to any set owner and are included in the newspaper radio and television listings.

One serious problem is that only very limited air time, especially for television, is available, since the Open University has no channel of its own. Its lectures have to be fitted into slots between BBC-2's entertainment programs, and each one has to be squeezed down to twenty-five minutes, which isn't long enough. The times are bound to be inconvenient to many students.

Mr. Gellan was disappointed that only 35 percent of the students were women—yet the main broadcast times are certainly awkward for them, at least for married women: 5:25 to 7:30 on weekdays, the normal time for preparing dinner, and Saturday mornings, when the children are home.

It's possible to watch a soap opera while basting the chicken or putting on galoshes, but not a lecture on Kant or comparative physiology. The Open University needs *much* more broadcasting time, and they'll have to get it, preferably by having their own TV channel. Domestic satellites and cables, when they come, will be a big help.

I've watched many of the Open University lectures on television. None that I saw had the genius of either *Sesame Street* or the Kendrew molecular biology series, but all were considerably better than the average live university lecture. They are simply and inexpensively produced by the BBC, with budgets that are microscopic by the standards of most entertainment programs.

In fact, speaking only of money (and money is one of the main problems here), you need only the back of an envelope and two minutes to see why corners have to be cut. *Sesame Street*, remember, cost $8 million for one program, five times a week for twenty-six weeks. Open University's forty thousand students pay an average of less than $300 tuition a year (and, of course, there are many other expenses besides making films), and that's a total of $12 million. But instead of *one* course, like *Sesame*, the Open University in 1973 had forty-two courses and part courses and was preparing twenty-two more for the 1974 academic year. It's a miracle they've done as well as they have.

True, many of the lectures are scarcely more than a picture of the lecturer and interviews with a few people, something radio could do as well. They don't take enough advantage of the camera's ability to move around, to see things in close-up, to reveal, to demonstrate, to fascinate.

One lecture film that did do this, and do it well, involved a science course on Faraday and electromagnetism. We visited the Royal Institute where Faraday did his work, went into his room, had close-up looks at his manuscripts and pages of his published works. Then we went into the lecture theater and watched the lecturer, in close-up, repeat Faraday's experiments, some of them with the very equipment originally used. It was all clear, informative, and absorbing.

In another, on music, all the instruments of the orchestra were demonstrated, and analyzed entertainingly by Johnny Dankworth who had composed a piece of music designed to illustrate the points.

In an arts course a film demonstrated the influence of Rousseau on Goethe by doing a dramatization of a short work of Goethe's in English. Here we could have used much more time. A lecture on war and society was illustrated by a number of film clips, most of them from World Wars I and II. An education lecture considered the change in status of students as they advanced to higher scholastic levels. It used a number of film interviews with girl students.

My guess is that right now the administrators, lecturers, and tutors of the Open University are learning even more than their students. Teaching people at a distance is a vastly complex business. What they learn is going to help us all, because this kind of university, in one form or another, is certainly going to exist in many countries. Paradoxically, Great Britain, which is small and compact, needs it much less than areas where people are widely scattered, like northern Canada, Australia, Siberia, the Pacific Islands, and many parts of Africa and South America.

I don't think open universities will ever replace the campus variety. They'll act as a supplement, and the education material they develop will also become a part of the audiovisual libraries of all schools, not replacing teachers any more than the printing press has replaced them.

Already several American universities are studying and testing the Open University's methods and materials, among them Rutgers, Maryland, the San Diego division of the University of California, and Princeton's Educational Testing Service.

The future possibilities for America are enormous. Imagine what would happen if all the state universities, for instance, were to combine to create a nationwide American Open University. Broadcasting could be by separate channel or by domestic satellite combined with cable TV. Courses would be prepared by the nation's best lecturers, including Nobel laureates, and produced by our best educational film and television people, with companion texts, filmstrips, cassettes, and microfiches.

Students could have personal contacts with teachers of the universities' extension divisions. It might double the effectiveness of our educational system, and the teaching material could be used in developing countries all over the world. The speaking parts of this kind of material are often voice-over, which is easily changed into other languages, and even lip-synchronous speech can easily be dubbed, as it is today with almost all commercial television films.

And it's not only those who haven't had university educations who will want to take American Open University courses. With all that exploding knowledge we may all want to be taking at least one course, all the time.

The Perpetual Education Plan

We may have to change our whole concept of education. We won't be able to stop teaching people in their early twenties; we may have to keep on learning, formally, all our lives. The distinction between students, teachers, and professionals will be wiped out, and all of us may have to play all three roles all our lives. To stop learning at any point would lead (as it has today) to doctors, scientists, engineers, and other professionals with obsolete educations.

Let's project the education of a young person in the (hopefully) very near future. We'll use the pronoun "he" and call him George, but everything will apply to both sexes, and the process would be the same for men and women.

Young Dr. Malone (Near-Future Model)

George's preschool education will surely include several programs of the *Sesame Street* sort. One of them will teach him a foreign language, and there will be a choice of several, perhaps French, German, Spanish, Russian, and Chinese. His family has a form of cable TV with about thirty channels. These nursery language programs will make no attempt to teach grammar; they will teach fluency just as a child learns his own language. There are games and singing and animated cartoons, and little stories, and puppets, all done in pure native accents. By the time he's five, he'll be able to speak and understand the language and even read a bit of it.

George goes off to school at five, and there he'll have more audiovisual material, in color and on a screen covering most of the wall. He'll have teaching machines, too. In spite of all the electronic innovations, there will actually be *more* teachers per child than there were in the olden days. From the very beginning the children will be encouraged to help each other—they will, in fact, begin almost at the start to teach. Everyone will teach a little all through his life.

George's school won't be separate from all other people, as schools were in his father's day. Part of the big, bright building is allocated to businesses and professions, with glass walls looking out on the school corridors, so that the children can see in. In George's school there's a broadcasting station, a newspaper office (it prepares the neighborhood paper which is printed, and also sent by facsimile over the cable to most homes), a computer service (George's home and many others in the neighborhood are connected to it), a metalworking shop, a veterinarian's (George's nose is pressed to the glass quite often here), a bakery, a market greenhouse, an architect's office, and even a live painter and sculptor. At certain times the children are allowed into all these places and can ask questions—so that all these professional people are really part-time teachers.

From about twelve to fifteen, or the junior high school stage, several hours a week are devoted to a series of "sample" courses, each lasting about a month. Many great universities and some of the most skillful teachers have helped to prepare these. All the programs are designed to fascinate as well as to inform. There will be courses in (really, more like visits to) chemistry, physics, biology, geology, psychology, and perhaps oceanography, astronautics, agriculture, electronics, mechanical engineering, surveys of music and the arts, sociology, and government. They will be done in every possible way, with cassettes and holography, but also with live teaching, laboratory participation, field trips, and visits from professionals.

There may be documentaries of the lives of people in all professions, and often these people will come to talk to them and answer questions. The object is to show the students the great range of knowledge, because soon they'll have to begin specializing. Today most children don't know what they "want to do," because they don't really know what's there.

George finds he's interested in sciences, and especially biology, so he branches off to more advanced sample courses in these. He talks to biologists and doctors and decides he'll go into medicine. In high school he concentrates on premedical courses, does well in them, and obtains his high school diploma.

At the age of eighteen he enters the profession of medicine. During his entire life he will never stop being a student, but at this point he also becomes a professional man, with a salary, at first very modest, but enough so that he can marry, if he wants, and have a small house or apartment near the medical complex.

In the beginning he spends about two thirds of his time studying medicine, and about one third working in the hospital, perhaps in the capacity of an orderly or some similar post. Each year he does slightly more intelligent work and assumes more authority.

After about five years of this routine he will receive his first degree, a "bachelor of medicine," and perhaps he is called, as surgeons are now in England, "Mr." Malone. He will already be doing some teaching, perhaps in the laboratory, instructing groups of younger students in dissection and the preparation of microscope slides. He will already be performing some of the duties of a physician and perhaps assisting in operations.

In about two more years he will become a master of medicine, continuing to study, but performing, perhaps half-time, the duties of an intern.

A year or two later, he becomes a full-fledged doctor of medicine and will be able to choose whether he wants to stay at the hospital or go into private practice.

However, like all professional men, he will be expected to continue studying. They'll all have periods of combined vacation and refresher-study—in addition to a normal, private vacation. There will be pleasant campuses, providing sailing, swimming, skiing, or tennis for afternoons, and mornings for seminars, lab sessions, conferences, and presentation of professional papers and reports.

All professions will work out systems like this. For engineers, chemists, production managers, and electronics specialists there will be industrial-university-research complexes, in which all will be studying, working, and teaching—and they'll all have semivacations of study and sport.

In all likelihood, even more students than presently do so will go into pure science. These individuals will enter great research complexes associated with universities. There will certainly be close relationships between these and the research and development departments of industries.

Of course, there's always a chance this happy vision won't come true, and that we shall go on, blundering away, as we're doing now. In this case education may just continue to be another status symbol.

Today, already, we're reaching the point where swimming pools cannot be made much larger, and the length of cars has already begun to recede. The competitor-in-affluence has now discovered a new status poker chip: *"How long do your offspring stay in school?"*

We'll have conversations like this:

"Yes, Harry, I was just talking to my son. He's taking his sixth Ph.D. Junior will be forty next spring!"

"Only the sixth, Bill? My Buddy is on his eighth—and he's going to be a grandfather any day now!"

In our best families it may be possible for the kids to die of senility before they have a chance to use anything they've learned!

13

HOW TO CHANGE PEOPLE
Or, Don't monkey with man!
He's perfect, he is!

Everyone knows that man is the perfect being, the glorious end result of evolution, and there's no use trying to make him any better. In fact, any steps to change him are immoral, heretical, and doomed to failure. Just leave him alone, please.

Now, that may not be *your* idea of it, but chances are, if we took a vote, that side would win. The small group who think people can be improved would definitely be on the losing side.

I know—I've been there before. I wrote a science fiction novel once, *The Carefully Considered Rape of the World*, in which I made the radical assumption that there were beings far more intelligent than humans. They had once been as stupid as we are now, but they had consciously, over many millennia, directed their own evolution toward healthier, longer-lasting bodies and, especially, much higher intelligence.

As one of the superior beings said: "Evolution is like a raft, drifting on the sea, with no chart, and no purpose but survival. The first beings to steer it in a direction of their own choosing—these could be the first gods of the universe." (They had not had the benefit of our missionaries.)

They worshiped the God of Seed—the unborn god who would arise one day from their own loins; at the time he had not yet emerged, but they assumed (heretically, we thought) that they were ten times closer to him than we, since they were ten times as intelligent. They considered themselves, you see, to be sort of missionaries to *us*.

Naturally, these beings had a low opinion of humanity. As one of them said, perhaps tactlessly:

> You can never imagine what it is like to be me, any more than a rat can imagine what it is like to be you. I know exactly what it is to be you because I can link myself in series with a human brain. . . . I fail to understand why humans stay alive. . . . Your greatest pleasure is a variety of pain. You are a mass of aches and terrors and itches and pimples and smells, with rotting teeth and running noses and fallen arches and watery eyes and ringing ears and bloated guts. All this in your only moment of consciousness in all eternity. Personally I'd rather have the chirping brainlessness of your idiot nightingale than little flesh-tearing, pain-loving, fright-frozen, hobgoblin-filled brains like yours. And you aren't making the slightest effort to change, even though you now have all the tools at hand to start.

You must remember that this was the opinion of a hideous monster, and not necessarily that of the author. (My family are all Episcopalians.) But the human characters in the book, to say nothing of many readers, were horrified. The consensus seemed to be that it would be sinful and generally unthinkable to take any step that would make people really intelligent. They wanted to keep us as God made us—stupid, cruel, and holy.

However, for those of you who are immoral enough to read further, the tools really are at hand to improve people, if we want to use them. (Some of them, I'm sure, none of us would want to use.) In fact, just to show how fast these things move, a lot of new ideas have appeared that weren't even known to my super-genius from outer space. It's one of the risks of being an omniscient author.

The best summary of some of the latest people-improving ideas that I've seen is an account by Joshua Lederberg, the famous Stanford University geneticist, in the Fourteenth Nobel Symposium.[1] He calls the science of the perfection of man *orthobiosis*. The experiments he cites have been carried out mostly with animals, and Dr. Lederberg is in no hurry to have us use them all on humans.

Orthobiosis is really in three parts: *eugenics*, actually changing the germ cell, so that the improvements, if any, will be permanent and inherited; *euphenics*, or changing individuals without changing their genes, so that the improvement is not inherited; and *euthenics*, or changing man by changing his environment.

Extraordinary euphenic, or noninheritable, changes can be made, some by processes beginning before birth. For example, Professor F. Zamenhof and his team at the University of California injected pregnant rats and mice with pituitary growth hormone. The brains of the offspring were not only larger but contained a higher ratio of neurones and glial cells. They had better brains, and they were more intelligent.[2] Would this create human geniuses? No one's tried it yet.

"Genius fish" were created by transplanting additional brain tissue to embryos. So far this hasn't gone beyond fish, and no one claims it saved *them* from the frying pan. Who knows where this could lead?

"They say Johnny has an IQ of 235!"

"Not really fair, is it? He had a brain-shot two months before he was born. Accounts for his slightly pear-shaped head. Frightful trouble with hats."

One trick was tried, almost coincidentally, with humans, by Professor O. S. Heyns at the University of Witwatersrand, who made a special plastic enclosure for the abdomen and pelvis of pregnant women. It was pumped out to one fifth of atmospheric pressure for half an hour a day during the last ten days of pregnancy. The idea was to reduce pressure on Mama, but it seems to have affected the babies' intelligences; one of the toddlers was answering the telephone at thirteen months and speaking four languages at the age of three.

Why? The most plausible theory is that the lower pressure allowed more oxygen to reach the fetus, particularly its brain.[3] This line of research may have considerable possibilities for the future.

Having trouble with organ transplants? Is your immune reaction throwing out your new liver or your new heart? It may be too late to do anything about you now, but it may be possible to have your embryonic children "vaccinated" with pooled, purified human tissue antigens. Then they won't reject any spare parts, as long as they're genuine *human* parts.

"George is getting a new heart! He's already got brand-new kidneys!"

"No problem—he had the antigen shots while he was still a gleam in Mama's eye. He can change anything. He may live forever."

"When he's changed *everything*, will he still be George?"

Enormous work is being done on immune reactions, and it's a good bet that the problem will be solved for all of us in the near future, and then there'll be spare parts for everyone—if we can find enough parts.

All the above changes are temporary, as far as the race is concerned. Not so with eugenics, the breeding of better humans. Lederberg feels that merely selective breeding (as we do with domestic animals) may not be sufficient to create any real changes. After all, animal breeders have two advantages—they can throw out the rejects, and they can use inbreeding. Once a breeder arrives at a really good thing—say, a cow that gives 20 percent more milk—he can stabilize the breed (or make sure it continues in offspring) by inbreeding. In humans we'd call it incest. The cows don't mind, but we tend to be touchy about going to bed with the immediate family.

Herman Muller and Julian Huxley have suggested a variation of selective breeding called germinal choice,[4] and it is entirely possible technically to do this today. Suppose you're a really transcendent genius, like Einstein or Newton or Beethoven, and are willing, if asked nicely, to provide semen for breeding. It would be a shame, really, to let the line die out or to limit it to three or four children. With artificial insemination you could become the father of thousands of children.

But just suppose that all these women have volunteered to bear your sons and daughters, have been impregnated, and the children are born and—alas!—you go crazy or show evidence of having some terrible hereditary flaw. (Of course, every normal marriage runs this risk.) To avoid such a thing, your semen is frozen, and it can be kept for many years, even long after your death. By this time, geneticists can make a calm judgment, and women volunteering to bear your children would be surer of genetic quality than any bride with a live husband has ever been. And it would be possible for a female child of this union to be "incestuously" impregnated with your semen, if that were genetically, morally, or otherwise desirable. This might, however, make for some odd relationships:

"Well, why shouldn't Harry be bright? Isaac Newton is his father—and also his grandfather!"

Note to transcendent geniuses: This can start for you today, if you like. Stop in at your neighborhood AI (artificial insemination) center. They'll take it from there. No telling *how* many kids you'll have in the twenty-first century! And not one will ever ask you for the keys to the car.

Science fiction writers, including me, have fiddled for years with the idea of working on the DNA molecule, the double helix that carries all our genetic information. Genetic engineering like this is called algeny, though no one as yet has really done it. Theoretically possible, it would be unimaginably difficult. Each DNA molecule (and you could put a million or so on the head of a pin) contains over a *billion* nucleotide information bits. All we have to do is find out what each nucleotide stands for, and then how to rearrange them in a better order. It is almost certain that no one will ever get in there with some kind of super-microscopic monkey wrench, but the ingenuity of man is infinite, and Nobel laureate Max Perutz, of Cambridge, is already suggesting "transduction," or introducing harmless viruses to carry genetic messages into the DNA spiral.[5] But not by tomorrow afternoon.

How to Repeat Yourself

The ultimate of narcissism is wanting to repeat yourself—to make more and more of *you*. This is not possi-

ble with sexual reproduction because—alas for narcis-
sists—this involves getting someone else into the act,
and therefore diluting (by about 50 percent) the true
essence of *you* in any offspring. Pity.

The way around this is known as *cloning*, making
identical copies of people. This has already been done
successfully with frogs (though it wasn't the frog's
idea), and it will certainly be possible soon to do it
with humans. The principle is the same; it's just that
the human ovum is much smaller than a frog's egg, so
it's more difficult. We're not even sure it *should* be
done with humans, but the results would certainly be
startling.

Clones would be as similar to each other as identical
twins, and for the same reason: they have exactly the
same genetic code—identical twins because they came
from the same ovum, which divided.

Making clones is like growing roses from cuttings
rather than seeds. You'll always get the same rose. In
normal conception the genes from the sperm join those
of the egg to form a new combination, and thus a different human being, with characteristics from both parents. To make a clone of *you*, the doctor would take a
single cell from you (not a reproductive cell, but almost any other kind, perhaps from a fingertip) and by
means of microsurgery remove the nucleus. He then
removes the nucleus from a human egg cell, replaces it
with your nucleus, and implants this egg in the womb
of a woman. It could be the same woman from whom
the egg originally came or another woman. From then

on the pregnancy and birth would be like any normal one.

The result would be another *you*, an identical copy. This way (if we had got cells from them in time) we could have made identical copies of Galileo, Newton, Mozart, Da Vinci, or whomever, and in any quantity desired. And from any of *them* further "cuttings" (i.e., single cells) can be made, and so on, making it possible to keep any extraordinary human a part of the human race (or many parts of it) for generations, or almost forever.

The only limiting factor (or, why not do everybody that way?) is that eventually the clones might, as Lederberg says, fall prey to "the accumulation of new mutations without the constant filtering of natural selection against homozygotes."[6] This is simply the normal screening process of evolution, eliminating the unfit. In other words, there's still a place for sex in the scheme of things, thank goodness. And, of course, there's no reason why the clones (who are perfectly normal humans) can't marry normally and have children, like anybody else.

British Professor J. B. S. Haldane suggested that after the age of fifty-five, great geniuses would spend their time educating their clonal offspring.[7]

And Lord Rothschild, the Cambridge physiologist, thought one problem was that too many people would want to clone themselves, as a kind of personal immortality.[8] How could it be limited? Should we allow a thousand Rasputins, a thousand Hitlers? Could an oil millionaire decide to make a few hundred copies of himself?

One suggested advantage of cloning is that clones might all have an uncanny psychological bond between them. Identical twins seem to have this—a way of communicating without words, almost by telepathy. Suppose, then, that a scientific institute included perhaps a thousand Einsteins linked in this kind of cerebral series. Their brain power might be considerably greater than that of the sum of the individuals. Almost any team or group activity, whether athletic, scientific, commercial, or artistic, could benefit. Imagine an orchestra of Toscaninis, a cloned baseball team, spaceship crew, or a commando of environmental experts. For once, committee thinking might work!

> BILL-ONE: Have you got point four, Bill-Three?
> BILL-THREE: I'm already on point six, Bill-One.
> BILL-TWO: Don't worry, boys, I've got it finished.
> BILL-FOUR: And I've Telexed the orders. Tennis, anyone?
> BILL-THREE: It's getting monotonous, though. When we play doubles with The Others, we always win, and when we play with each other, we can never get beyond deuce!

A further advantage would be that each clone would share the same immune-reaction and could accept spare parts from the others, just as identical twins do now. Hearts, lungs, kidneys, livers, any part from any brother or sister clone killed in an accident, could be frozen and kept until one of the others needed it. It would give them all a great sense of security.

We can even imagine the evil genius who has clones of himself made, only so that he can keep them in a kind of private reserve, to be freshly killed, as a personal spare-parts bank.

Cloning could be a part of the "germinal choice" program, as mentioned above, allowing the original genius to live out his life first before massive cloning—thus making sure he had no hidden biological fault. His cells could be kept alive, or just one or two clonal offspring born. Then, after his death at a ripe old age, mass production could start.

And to make the almost unimaginable leap—let's assume that your brain, or even parts of your brain, including some of your memory, could be transferred (when you are, say, sixty-five or seventy, or perhaps immediately before your death—your *first* death) into the head of a young clone, of you. It should be accepted biologically. Would you, yourself, then be transferred? What *is* "self" but memory? Might your memory (and thus yourself) then blend into the newer brain, in a kind of personal and biological Nirvana? The process could presumably be continued for generations. Would that be immortality? Would your education, or part of it, and your experience and skills be transferred as well? Would the young clone that you have entered be able, for example, to ski if he had never done it before? Would he suddenly know Chinese or how to play the violin?

In other, more intimate activities, the complexities could be dazzling, or even embarrassing:

"Oh, Johnny, do that again, darling! Whatever happened to you?"

"Well, ever since my operation—"

"Don't lie to me, Johnny! You've been with other women!"

"Actually, I've been with dozens of them, darling—"

"*Dozens*! You get right out of this bed, you, you—"

"But not *really* with any of them, I mean—"

"I never want to see you again!"

"Never?"

"Never! But please do that once more, will you, darling?"

After all, you'd think *any* skill would be transferred, wouldn't you? Just imagine the experience of an old roué and the body (and endurance) of a young Apollo. Would any woman be safe? It might give natural selection quite a boost.

On the other hand, cloning may lead to numerous problems in the home. Suppose an ambitious mother married to, perhaps, a truck driver has volunteered for cloning and has given birth to Einstein-678, now perhaps seven years old:

"You leave him alone, Harry! He's Einstein!"

"You're his mom, right?

"Yes, Harry."

"That makes me his old man. How did Einstein get in there?"

"He's a clone, Harry."

"I don't care if he's an ice cream clone. What'd he do with my *Popular Mechanics*?"

"Harry, who needs it? He's reading Jack Monod in French!"

"Tell him to come here!"

"He's down playing with Mr. Gorgan's computer, with one of his brothers, Einstein-685."

"His *brothers*? Are you holdin' out on me Mabel?"

It may even break up homes.

Suppose you could plant your memory, or part of it, into the brain of one of your clones. Why not into *several* of them? What would happen then? Would you be "you" in several places at once? Exactly what is *you*, anyway? And surely, if this were possible, and a number of "yous" were walking around, one or more of them would always survive. Would this, too, be immortality?

Certainly this, or some other kind of spare-parts immortality, or at least enormous longevity, will be possible within a relatively short time. In other words, some people will be able to live practically forever. How do we decide which ones?

How to Be Chosen

This problem, how to be chosen, is already a serious one. It can be done—but will they do it for me?

The issue is especially contentious in spare-parts surgery. Who gets the new kidney? Even more often, now, the question is "Who gets to use the kidney machine?"

In England, for instance, where money is not as determining a factor in medical decisions as it is in some other countries, the choice has less to do with the ability to pay, and doctors find themselves having to make life-and-death decisions: there are five kidney machines available in this area, and we have ten people who are sure to die if they don't have one immediately. Which five shall we choose? Shall we save Mrs. A., thirty-five, mother of four young children, rather than Mr. B., forty-six, father of two almost-grown sons, and also a valuable engineer? Usually anyone over fifty will have to yield to a younger person. Five people will have to be condemned to death. Which five? And who decides? Of course, before the invention of the machine, all ten would have died.

There will be more and more of this. It will be possible to save Mr. C., but it will cost half a million dollars to do it. Can we afford it? What is a person worth? Is it better to save a fifty-one-year-old widower than to build, perhaps, a new clinic for children? Let him die, then?

Up to now the choice has been the responsibility of doctors. In a democracy should there be some kind of jury? Will a person, or his advocate, be allowed to (or even required to) present his case to a jury? Why should I be saved? Actually, why should I be saved rather than, say, Miss D.? It might mean another twenty or thirty years of life—and during that time (at the speed we're going) we may discover something *re-*

ally miraculous, and the twenty or thirty might really be a great deal more, and after that, who knows?

Steps You Can Take

Let us assume that you are convinced of your value to society. Then how do you go about saving yourself—saving yourself for others, of course? How do you convince the local County Immortality Board that you are as worthy as you think you are?

You'll have to be on your guard against Future Dastards and their Immortality Lawyers, who may try to elbow their way ahead of you with appeals, perhaps, to naked emotion.

Perhaps the only tenable attitude is one of simple heroism and self-sacrifice:

"No, no, don't save me! Let my work die with me."

"What work?"

"Not a word yet on paper. It's all in *here!*"

"Give us a sample."

"It's not for today! It's for tomorrow. I'm ahead of my time. Let the world wait!"

Once you're on the way to immortality, make sure that everyone is glad that you're the one who got saved.

How to Order Your Children

Even before practicable, everyday immortality, we'll have the option of ordering children of our choice. Today, we just insert the nickle, spin the wheels, and hope we can hit the jackpot. This slot-machine method will not be good enough for the future.

We're already right on the threshold of predetermination of sex. A great deal of progress has been made here, partly because of research in breeding dairy herds. Since one bull can handle scores of cows, the object is to produce mostly female calves. Want a girl first, and then a boy? Put in your order.

With artificial insemination, cloning, laboratory-cultured and biologically engineered embryos (beginning, that is, outside the womb) and genetic cells programmed with synthetic messages brought in by viruses —all things that biological engineers are sure will come in a few decades,[9] it should be possible for parents (if you can still call them that) to order their children with as many "factory options" as a Chevrolet.

You may choose to have your child a clone of some future Einstein or Beethoven, and you may also be able to specify a personalized model. He doesn't have to *look* like Einstein.

"Now, what hair colors do you have?"

"Here's our hair-color chart, madam, with a choice of twenty-six shades. The metallic ones are a little more."

"That red is nice."

"Definitely 'in' this year, madam. Usually comes with a modified freckle. Now, what about noses?"

"My husband insists on the Jones nose, with a little *whooops* here—and he said to make sure the boy is six foot six. Basketball, you know."

"For basketballers we're doing a special six-foot-nine model—"

"Let me check our doorways for clearance."

Tomorrow's World of Sport

Everyone feels that the first practicable, commercial clone will be a racehorse. Assume that the greatest racehorse of all time, who has won ten million dollars, breaks a leg or becomes too old to run. Put him at stud, naturally, but his offspring will never be quite the same, diluted always by other blood. Clones, of course! Mares, dozens of them, will be implanted with cloned ova, and the horseplayers will go crazy:

"How do you bet it, Joe? There's five Secretariats in the third race, and three more in the fourth! Every race is a three-way photo finish!"

People-sport is sure to follow. Clones will certainly be made of the great champions of all sports. What worries some of the future-seers is that we won't stop there.

Everyone knows how serious the Olympics are becoming. They are beginning to take the place of war as a proving ground for national superiority and ideological one-upmanship. The East Germans, for one, have practically converted their country into an athlete factory.

Where will we stop?

Professor Lederberg thinks it quite possible (though

he doesn't like the idea) that human nuclei may be implanted in animals, creating hybrids, and that even organs and limbs of humans and animals may be interchanged.[10] The possibilities of some of these wonders won't be lost on our Olympic committees, if the games continue to escalate.

Perhaps it would be something like this:

The 2040 Olympic games really began in the genetics factories in the early years of the century. Everyone knew that if we were to break the two-and-a-half-minute mile (actually the 1500 meters) or the five-second 100, that genetic engineering would have to give our athletes a helping hand, or test tube.

What was happening was top secret. The "sweatsock" labs, as they were called, were closely guarded. And even then they were penetrated by daring genetic spies.

Everyone remembered the charges and countercharges made at earlier games, especially in the 1950s and 1960s, about the virile-looking women athletes. Were they really women? When does a girl cease to be a girl? Inject a woman with enough male hormone and her muscles will be larger and more masculine. She may even have to begin shaving—but she still has her female sex organs, more or less. In any case, rules were made and sex tests carried out in subsequent games. At least no out-and-out man would be allowed to compete in women's events. The geneticists were told to make sure there was no fiddling around with sex.

"But except for that, boys, full speed ahead! We

want our kids to be the best kids in the world! Nothing is too good for our kids!"

The games themselves were an absolute revelation. Records not only fell—they were pulverized. The human, or practically human, race had never been so proud of itself.

The results are history, and the pictures were sent in full-color holography to all neighboring planets. However, perhaps a few bits of dialogue, recorded here and there around the Olympic Village, will best give the tone and feeling of these really incomparable games of 2040:

"Good? Desmond is the greatest middle distance runner in history! Who else has won an Olympic gold medal—*and* the Kentucky Derby! He can run with or without a jockey. Just point him in the right direction!"

"I hear the Aussies had this great girl high jumper."
"Great? She qualified with two kids in her pouch! What they got her on was shaving."

"Is your free style champ really a descendant of Mark Spitz?"
"I don't care who his grandfather is! He just swam upstream to spawn!"

"What happened to your sprinter?"

"They wouldn't let him use his electric rabbit."

"They say your girl backstroker flunked her sex test."

"Communist lies! Her problem is, they can't decide which is her back."

"Sure, Phoebe's gills are legal. It's just that she talks in a baritone."

There are always critics, but everyone agreed that the national honor was at stake, and they certainly did play "The Star-Spangled Banner" a lot. And, as one of the coaches said later, "If you want to break the two-minute mile, you gotta make compromises someplace."

How to Have Our Own Home-Grown Planet of Apes

As you can see, genetic changes aren't always for the better, but in the future it will certainly be possible to improve the intelligence, general health, and longevity of any animal, even the human animal.

We've been using eugenics for decades to improve chickens and dairy cows—not for intelligence, only for groceries. Anyone can see how we've improved the breasts of turkeys; we could have improved their minds, as well. It's just that we don't like turkeys for their minds.

But I fear it will be a long time before we start to

improve humans. There are so many taboos, perhaps some of them necessary.

Meanwhile, the scientists are going to keep on working with animals. Let's suppose that a special effort is made with chimpanzees, and every biological device is used to improve them genetically. They are tested for intelligence, and only the most intelligent 3 or 4 percent are selected in each generation for breeding, and these multiplied by artificial insemination and ovulation (i.e., eggs from the most intelligent females implanted in the others). Some of the genetic cells will be programmed with synthesized information. Germinal choice and cloning are used, freezing and preserving both semen and cells for cloning.

Little by little the intelligence of the chimpanzees rises until one day, perhaps centuries later, it surpasses that of men. At this point they decide to direct the process themselves, and not having our biological taboos, multiply their intelligences still further. Finally they become truly godlike creatures, infinitely superior to today's men—or to tomorrow's man, if he is allowed to remain (as he now is) in a biological backwater, either staying the same or retrogressing.

Would they take over the planet to run it better than we have been doing, perhaps protecting us in pleasant human preserves, trying to curb our perennial tendency to kill each other?

The super-chimps could still, if they liked, look like chimpanzees, and probably would, since they would regard chimpanzees as beautiful. On the other hand, they

could arrange to look like anteaters or, if they pre-
ferred, they could make all their male folk look like
Rudolph Valentino, and all their females like Marilyn
Monroe.

Curb That Crocodile

We could, of course, do the same thing with humans.
We shall certainly take *some* people-improving steps.
How far will we go?

The question for biologists now is not "Is it possible
to improve man?"—every competent biologist knows it
is possible. The only questions are "Should we?" and
"In what direction?"

The popular assumption is that man is perfect, or at
least could be *made* perfect; it's just a matter of vitamins and education. Few biologists agree.

Even our brains, of which we're so proud, are pretty
rickety. Arthur Koestler believes there's really some
screw loose, since we're the only animal that seems bent
on self-destruction. He cites all the archaeological evidence of our odd impulses toward human sacrifice and
the fact that we're just about the only animals that kill
their own kind.

Koestler quotes Dr. MacLean (of the Papez-Mac-
Lean theory of emotions) on the three-tiered structure
of our mongrel brains:

> Man finds himself in the predicament that Nature has
> endowed him essentially with three brains. . . . the

> oldest of these brains is basically reptilian. The second has been inherited from lower mammals, and the third is a late mammalian development. . . . We might imagine that when the psychiatrist bids the patient to lie on the couch, he is asking him to stretch out alongside a horse and a crocodile.[11]

Maybe we can keep the horse, but we'll have to curb that crocodile!

The biggest question, which will be with mankind far into the future, is "If we're going to improve man, what shall we improve him *into?*" And also, "Who shall decide this?"

Aldous Huxley, satirizing this sort of thing in *Brave New World*, feared that we might make several different *kinds* of humans, of varying degrees of intelligence —almost of varying degrees of stupidity. And we could certainly do this, technically. The lowest of Huxley's clone groups would be suited only for such occupations as elevator operators, and would be happy doing this. Huxley's vision has already gone out of date. (Woe betide anyone who writes about the future!)

We already have more really stupid, unskilled people than we need, since automation runs the elevators and does increasing amounts of that kind of work. What we need now is skilled technicians, to keep the automation running. Our stupidest people have nothing to do except collect their relief checks and make love—thereby creating vast numbers more of the stupidest people, to help move our evolution backward.

Some feel we should breed specialists; i.e., special

hybrid super-musicians, super-poets, and super-scientists. This would almost certainly lead to music that no one but musicians could understand or would want to hear, and poetry that no one but super-poets could fathom—a situation that is developing already with our present (i.e., normally, humanly stupid) composers and poets.

As for scientists, as C. P. Snow keeps telling us, they're already so far beyond the reach of most of us that we can no longer detect them with our naked brains. (Try reading, as I've been doing lately, the really far-and-away scientific journals; it is said that our scientific knowledge now doubles every five years; I can believe it.)

My hunch is to opt for uniformly high quality for everyone; wipe out all the genetic handicaps and inherited diseases; give us a good, long, healthy-mature period (say, a hundred years?) and a reduced (if not abolished) period of senility, combined with a stable, well-adjusted intelligence of, for a start, the equivalent of today's IQ of 200, for all, and a breeding out of our tendencies toward violence and cruelty and domination. Then, let the new world full of good-guy geniuses take it from there. Let them go back to floppy old *us* if they want to. Would you like to bet whether they would?

It can all be done with the technical knowledge we have right now, and even without the DNA monkey wrench.

Do you want to bet whether we'll start soon? Of all

the dreams of the future, the perfectibility of man is the one that terrifies us the most. Every time I bring it up, people run away screaming. So run away and scream. But don't worry, it will never even begin to happen in your time or mine.

We'd rather destroy the earth than improve mankind.

14

HOW TO CHANGE YOUR MIND

Can we save the world by
putting our heads in a box?

There's another answer to the question "Shall we improve people?" The answer is "There isn't time." It takes a long time to improve people genetically. Entire generations are involved, and we haven't time for generations. We hardly have any time at all.

"Are we doomed then?" you ask.

"Well, yes, as free people. If you want to be saved, then freedom is definitely out."

"You mean we can't do what we want anymore?"

"Oh, yes, you will do what you want to do. It's just that you won't *want* to do what you want to do now because we will make you want to do what *we* want you to do."

Is that Big Brother talking? Well, not exactly. It's the People Conditioners talking, the fellows who want to help us by changing our minds.

The People Conditioners have noticed, as so many others have, that the end of the world is upon us, and that the way around it is to redesign our culture because, as Professor B. F. Skinner of Harvard says, a culture that is not designed to survive is one that is not well designed.[1] It is hard to disagree with that point.

And what the conditioners mean by redesigning a culture is that they want to redesign *you*. Not all of you, just your head. You might say it is a kind of benevolent brain washing. Of course, in brain washing, as in beauty, benevolence is in the eye of the beholder, or actually the conditioner. They want to do it for your good, and they are pretty sure what your good is.

"Exactly What Is *a People Conditioner?"*

To understand People Conditioners, you first must understand psychologists, and it is very easy to misunderstand them because of the way they talk.

It is essential to remember that psychology started out a very short time ago because somebody thought there ought to be a science about the brain, especially the human brain. I thought so, too, and began to study it at the university. I discovered, as everyone else did, that nobody really knew anything about the human brain yet, though they were all trying to find out. So they had to make up for it by creating a complicated vocabulary because otherwise everything would seem so obvious.

Psychologists discovered that if a person put out his hand and you pricked it with a pin, the person would pull his hand back. If you told students this, they would laugh. But if you called the person a *subject*, and the pin prick a *stimulus*, or even an *aversive stimulus*, and the pulling back of the hand a *reaction*, then the students wouldn't laugh; they would solemnly write down the words. That gave the whole thing a scientific basis.

In fact, if you did this to the subject, who was usually a student, often enough he would decide not to come into the laboratory to have his hand pricked, and he would become a *conditioned student*. He was conditioned to stay away from the laboratory. It really isn't any more complicated than that, though of course with the right words you can make it as complicated as you wish. You might even say I became a conditioned student. I got conditioned to study something else.

Well, if you could find enough unconditioned students, you could perform the pin-pricking experiment thousands of times, write it all down and make graphs about it, and pretty soon you had a literature.

In the last forty years or so, psychologists have learned a great deal more about the human brain, and even though they haven't given up those words, they are trying to do a lot to help us all and save the world.

There are really two kinds of psychologists, behaviorists and "the other kind." Since my professor was a behaviorist (his god was Watson, at that time the most behaviorist of all), he called the other kind armchair psychologists because they just sat in their armchairs and thought about the human brain, with *their* human brains, of course. They were right in the middle of their material. Behaviorists got up out of their armchairs and pricked hands and shocked rats and fed pigeons. Except that you could be thrown out of the union for saying you fed a pigeon. What you did was *reinforce* it with food.

Professor B. F. Skinner is, of course, the most famous living behaviorist and pigeon reinforcer. Pigeons, like people, can be made to do anything a pigeon or a person *can* do if you keep them hungry enough and feed them—pardon, reinforce them—when they do what you want.[2]

Skinner made pigeons walk a figure eight and play Ping-Pong and even guide (and ride) a bomb to a target. The pigeon was trained to watch a TV screen inside the bomb and keep on pecking at the image of the target. It really worked, though Skinner could never get anybody to believe it would. You see, the pigeon was conditioned to think he was doing this for his own good. Behaviorists always try to do everything for everyone's own good, but you can see from this that it works just as well when the subject gets blown to smithereens—as long as he doesn't *know* he is going to get blown to smithereens.

One of Professor Skinner's biggest contributions was to condition pigeons automatically, in the now-famous Skinner Box, which can reinforce a pigeon when he (Skinner, that is) isn't even there, though the pigeon

has to be there. Every time the pigeon pecks at an il-
luminated disk (or whatever Skinner wants it to do) it
is automatically reinforced with corn.

The idea works on rats, monkeys, or almost anything,
including people, though it is harder and harder to
find people who will get inside. The next best thing
is a teaching machine, which Professor Skinner has
invented, too. You don't have to get inside a teaching
machine. At least so far you don't.

How to Start People Pigeon-Pecking

You could certainly argue, and Professor Skinner
does, that if the only way to save the world is to condition people, then we'd better get right at it.

Since I have a head start on conditioning, being a
conditioned student, plus practical experience out in
the world, I decided to get right into this and try to
help Professor Skinner. The first thing I did was to
start listening to symphony music while doing something else, the way Professor Skinner does, and that
helped a lot. It sort of mixes up your mind, and I think
that's what you need here.

Then I read *Beyond Freedom and Dignity* twice, including the small print, and though the deep thinking
is all in there, Professor Skinner doesn't say anywhere
what we should actually start doing to save the world,
except that we should start doing it right away. We all
agree with that part.

So what we have to do here is to turn this into applied psychology, or applied Skinner. Applied psychology is the vocational, or workaday, or *I'm Okay— You're Okay*, branch of the subject. It's like plumbing is to hydraulics.

We Skinner-plumbers are going to have to rough out our own model of Skinner Box society, and our preliminary studies indicate that the most important thing about people conditioning is to get in on the ground floor.

In this new Skinner world there are going to be, basically, two kinds of people: the people *inside* the Skinner Boxes and the people *outside* of them. Now, Professor Skinner says the people inside should be the same as the people outside, but this is easier said than done, and is complicated by the fact that the boxes aren't *really* boxes (for people, that is; they're *really* boxes for pigeons). They are mental boxes, which puts the inside and the outside on a now-you-see-it, now-you-don't basis. We are going to assume for this applied exercise that we are the people who are more outside than inside, because we are the ones who are building the boxes. Just keep remembering that psychology is really very simple; it's only the words that get complicated.

How to Condition Your Wife

You have to walk before you can run, and the best way to start is at home. You can do it yourself. Anyone who can roller-paint the rumpus room or lay kitchen linoleum can do home conditioning. Start by conditioning your wife, and then you can help all of us with society in general.

> *Note to female readers*: This works equally well for husbands. It just depends on who is inside the box and who is outside. Stay outside, metaphorically speaking, and keep him firmly inside. This will work even if he thinks he is outside and you are inside, and thinks he is conditioning *you* at the same time.

Think, first, of the advantages of a really properly trained woman (or man). This can be accomplished, Professor Skinner assures us, *without actually punishing them* at all. It is merely a system of rewards—and, of course, of withholding rewards, too.

The first step is to decide what you want to condition your wife *into*. The way these things are always set up, it is the one outside the box who is driving. After all, it was Skinner who thought about walking in figure eights, not the pigeon. It's the sort of thing that would never occur to a self-respecting pigeon.

However, if you like, you *can* train your wife to walk in figure eights. For a start, women do often go around in circles. Find out if she is basically a clockwise or a counterclockwise woman. If clockwise, reward (or reinforce) her every time she turns counterclockwise. There are all kinds of ways to reward women, and the better you know them, the more ways there are. Before you know it, you will have her doing figure eights:

"Darling, if you really *want* me to do another figure eight, I will. Gladly!"

This shows obedience. Actually, *responsiveness* is a more psychologically accurate word here. And though some figure eights are more interesting than others, you may find many even more useful things to train her to do. Just remember to reinforce her, this way or that, whenever she does something that pleases you. Before you know it, she will be pleasing you all the time.

Do *not* reward her when she does not please you. For example, if you do something nice for a baby every time he cries, you are conditioning him to cry. When Nixon's dog chewed the carpet, he gave the dog a bone to distract him. Kissinger, who was watching, said, "You have just taught your dog to chew carpets." This is true, and wives are just the same.

If your wife should start chewing the carpet, don't reward her. Should you, however, *punish* her? Well, to go back to dogs, some dog-conditioning authorities recommend not actually *hurting* the dog, but demonstrating disapproval by striking him noisily, but not painfully, with a rolled-up newspaper. This works well with dogs, though with wives it can become more complicated:

"Look, lover, if you're going to brain me with a paper, I'll thank you not to use that fascist [or communist] rag!"

Skinner, to his credit, is against punishment of all kinds, even with rolled-up newspapers, arguing that it merely motivates people to find ways to avoid it.

But in our rosy future, there will be many ways of showing mild disapproval of minor infractions that almost any careless wife (or husband) could commit. Here are several that will work much better than rolled-up newspapers:

The *muffled wail*. Almost any hi-fi amateur can set up remote-controlled tape and speaker systems. Locate a good muffled wail or stifled scream, and keep it where you can get at it:

"Oh, my goodness, Davey!"

"What's the matter, pet?"

"Didn't you hear that? It was almost like a—a muffled wail!"

"Heard it again, did you?"

"It just seems that every time I contradict you it happens."

"Somebody somewhere must be trying to tell you something, pet."

The mild shock treatment. Shock treatments are almost the bread and butter of some of our psychiatric establishments, and you can use them, too, with variations:

"Wooo-ooops, Davey!"

"More muffled wails, pet?"

"Didn't *you* feel that electric shock?"

"Where did you feel it, pet?"

"Where I sit down, that's where. It happened the minute I asked you to go down to the supermarket. It happened the last time, too."

"Gosh, things like that make you feel real humble, don't they?"

This sort of thing is referred to by the box-boys as

aversive reinforcement, or sign of disapproval. Only sticklers consider it a punishment.

Use a six- or twelve-volt transformer. Your object is guidance and betterment only.

The Reward Gambit

Rewards, too, have their place. Try using a system advocated by Skinner for delinquent boys—a merit-point scheme. When your wife pleases you, give her points, which can be added up and translated into real rewards.

"Oh, well done, pet! You've shined my shoes again! Ten points!"

"Ten whole points, really, Davey?"

"Twenty more and we'll think of something *very* nice for you!"

Future planners will work out something tangible, like a Green Stamp system, with something she can paste in her little book.

Experiment on your own! Remember that conditioning must suit the subject. Or, as Skinner says, "We must not overlook the control exerted by the pigeon." Skinner has often felt himself pigeon-controlled, and there are some who think it serves him right. During this occasionally tense period you, too, may occasionally feel pigeon-controlled, or in this case, wife-controlled, which is worse. As her character improves under your guidance, you, too, must improve along with her.

"Nature," said Francis Bacon, with Skinner's approval, "to be commanded must be obeyed." Once your wife is really conditioned, of course, it is she (or nature, in this context) who will obey you.

Soon you will have a wife who is obedient, cheerful, helpful, and respectful, quiet when you want peace, gay when you want joy. Keep on reinforcing her, and she will reinforce you. And if you have conditioned her properly, she will not only *be* like this, she will *want* to be.

Today Your Wife, Tomorrow the World

You're now ready to help us save the world, and our first step is to decide what to save the world *from*. We'll get no guidance from Skinner here; we're on our own.

By this time all of us are familiar with the basic doomsday threats, which boil down, roughly, to the three main hobgoblins: (1) too many people, (2) too much pollution, and (3) wasting of resources. And the last two would be much easier to handle if it weren't for all those people.

People are such a problem that the M.I.T. computer (to name only one) simply throws up its hands and says that if you just give them enough to eat, they're at it, and we all know what they're at. One trouble with computers, in this context, is that they don't know what they're missing.

"Can We Condition Sex Away?"

We can condition sex away to a certain extent, if we want to. In fact, very interesting studies have been carried out to recondition—if that's the word—male homosexuals.

Psychiatrists have taken consenting males (in this case, consenting to be psyched) and placed them in viewing rooms where they were shown, among other things, erotic pictures of men. The male pictures were accompanied by electric shocks, or horrible noises, or bad smells, or anything else that would make men seem sexually unpleasant. They were being conditioned against erotic masculinity, and we're told that it worked on some of them. Of course, not all of the poor chaps were then able to enjoy women. It just spoiled their enjoyment of men.

So, if you're a homosexual, you can see what we heteros are doing to bring fun into your life.

But we could use this method to reduce the population. All we have to do is condition heterosexuals against the opposite sex. It might even end the human race.

The Victorians tried to make sex go away by pretending it wasn't there, reducing the amount of visible human skin to the hands and face, even on the beach. The result of all this was the double standard (extramural fun for men only), a bonanza for brothels, *Fanny Hill*, and probably the largest families in history. You have to be careful when you mess around with sex.

The growing consensus is that the fun can stay. It is only the dangerous side effects (i.e., babies) that are the problem. In fact, unproductive sex is getting to be almost the only fun we can have without hastening the end of civilization. The old-fashioned Sunday drive in the country is, by the new rules, a highly sinful act, ecologically speaking, poisoning the air and wasting fossil fuel, whereas a sexual orgy (as long as it is kept babyless) is as environmentally innocent as knitting or reading a book. The new doomsday saint may harbor lascivious thoughts and even drink his fill, as long as he returns the bottle. And any canonical strictures against birth control, however well meant, are by the commandments of the new era the most sinful words of man.

For the future, then, our sex conditioning should concentrate on solutions like this:

The Magical Population-Reducing People Crib

This is quite different from the kiddy box, or air crib, that Professor Skinner invented, and it may even be that he has got the problem turned around the wrong way. Skinner's kiddy box was a glass-fronted cage with controlled temperature; just put the baby into it, wearing nothing but a diaper. Skinner put his own daughter into one, and she stayed there, naked and happy, until she was old enough to get out.

There is nothing really wrong with this procedure, but it doesn't attack the problem head on. We propose for the immediate future the people-conditioning adult crib, designed only to reduce the population.

If you are a young woman of child-bearing age who has not yet borne any (or at least not many), you would be shut up, as the only adult, in our People Crib, with a group of about twelve children ranging in age from eighteen months to four years. Children of this age, as all parents know, have the agility of orangutans and, as yet, low mental development. That is to say, they have lots of mobility and no sense. There will be no problem getting as many of these as we need. In fact, fees paid by donating women, or mothers, will finance the entire project, including subsequent psychiatric care for the subjects.

Any small house or apartment can be turned into a People Crib merely by sealing all exits after the subject and children have been admitted. It can be any shape or color, but should be comparatively indestructible, preferably waterproof, so that it can be hosed down daily, containing no sharp edges or breakable bric-a-brac above a five-foot level, or higher where climbing is possible. In fact, where climbing is possible, it should be made impossible.

No communication would be allowed between the subject and any intelligent being (i.e., any human over the age of four) except for one telephone call daily from the man of her choice. This must, by prior agreement, last no longer than ninety seconds, and must always end with the words "Gotta go now, baby! Big meeting! Have fun with the kids!"

Conditioning hours will last from 8:00 A.M. until 7:00 P.M., during which time all needs, either real or imaginary, of the children (or stimuli) shall be tended to in one way or another by the subject. The children will all be chosen for vigorous health, physical strength, vocal power, and insistent qualities, and evenly distributed as to motor types: i.e., clinging, grabbing, climbing, and lie-down-on-the-floor-and-kick-and-scream types, and would include children who hate other children, and children who hate people.

After ten days of this, the subject would be given several days of psychiatric treatment and convalescence and would then be offered a comprehensive course in all modern methods of birth control.

Some future planners feel that all men of child-conceiving age (this is just about everybody over thirteen) should be given the People Crib treatment as well, or as much as they can stand.

Can the Pollution-Free Pigeon Help Us?

Population, then, is something we Applied-Skinner-Boxers are ready for. But what about pollution? Can people be conditioned not to pollute?

Like conditioners everywhere, we're thinking of this first in terms of pigeons, before going on to man himself. Both pigeon-wise and pollution-wise, we feel that figure eights are irrelevant in this area.

What *is* pigeon pollution, then? Condensing all the volumes that have been written about it into one line: To a pigeon, pollution is dropping things! And we all know what kind of things pigeons drop.

To change this might change the whole concept of pigeons. Think of Washington Square, Trafalgar Square, or Saint Marks in Venice. People could come out into the open again.

Once the pollution-free pigeon is a reality, we can march forward to pollution-free man.

And as to the wasting of natural resources, we are still trying to develop a pigeon that knows what a natural resource *is*.

In fact, those who haven't studied conditioning as much as we have tend to take an impatient attitude. As one of our typists said:

"Wouldn't it just be simpler to *explain* it to people?"

"*Explain* it to them?"

"I mean, telling them what would happen if they didn't stop polluting and all? I mean, you couldn't *do* that with a pigeon, could you?"

From this you can see how far we Applied-Skinner-Boxers have to go in our battle to help us save ourselves.

Super-Conditioning in the Symbiotic Super-Box

Suppose, however, that the real doomsday crunch arrives, and the powers of earth are persuaded by the

People Conditioners to use the ultimate conditioner, the Super-Box. The Skinner Boxes of today will be popguns compared with the heavy-artillery conditioners of the future.

Remember those computers that will be linked to the human brain? Now, carry that to the ultimate extreme—and if you know humans, that's where they'll carry it—and you'll have the Symbiotic Super-Box, and you'll be plugged in, and they won't like it if you pull the plug. In the ordinary symbiotic computer, you know what the computer is thinking, and it has a pretty good idea what *you're* thinking, too. Well, this one is also programmed to do something about it.

Let's say that you've stepped into (or been led into) the Company Happy Room, or Brain Refresher Station. It's only there to help you, to make you a Better Person, Our Kind of Person. The friendly Happy Room attendant plugs you in, and sort of straps you in, for your own protection. He puts the shiny little electrodes on your temples and asks you if they're comfortable and hooks up the recorder. They'll record your thoughts, too, just in case your supervisor wants to flip through your little mental quirks to help you.

He turns on the current, and right away your head is really swimming. If the computer disagrees with what you're thinking, it gives you (through those electrodes) either a mildly aversive warning jolt (*buzz!*) or (if you don't respond well to that) something just a bit more memorable (*zapp!*). If it approves, it will give you a mild pleasure impulse (*mmmm!*) or even something downright ecstatic (*wowie!*)—all depending, of course, on your thinking.

Let's suppose that the fellow in the next office has just been given an absolutely irresistible secretary, and you've just walked by her desk on your way to the Happy Room:

> You (*thinking*): Oh, what a doll! [*buzz!*] I don't care, jumping into bed with her would be worth— [*zapp!*] Yes, it's even worth—[*double zapp!!*] Oh, no, it's not worth that. Perhaps I should be thinking what a lovely company this is—[*mmmm!*] Oh, how nice! And how I can help my nice supervisor— [*mmmm! mmmm!*]—and increase the company's profits—[*wowie!*]

Before you know it you will become right-thinking, profit-oriented, constructive. Your possibilities for good will be unlimited. (And if you want to think those sexy thoughts, by all means wait till you're unplugged!)

Only for really stubborn and wrong-thinking employees would the truly *corrective*-type impulse be used (*double screamee!*) and it wouldn't have to be used often. Very soon all thought would be good, pure, and forward-thinking.

Would there, in such a thoroughly conditioned society, be no evil and no sin? Well, let's have a look at that whole wicked subject. . . .

15

HOW TO SIN IN THE FUTURE

*Or, Can we preserve our respectability
in a shameless world?*

In the future, under any circumstances, you will surely want to keep your respectability and preserve a high moral tone.

Now, this may be more difficult than you think. There is a possibility that unless we act quickly, there may be no sin in the future. What, then, will become of respectability?

After all, respectability is a feeling of moral superiority, and you can't be "better" unless somebody is "worse." It's as difficult to imagine respectability without sin as it is to conceive of silence if there were no noise.

Already the position of sin is badly eroded. Old, formerly upstanding sins like pride and sloth and gluttony can hardly hold up their heads as modern and relevant. Virtually all of today's sin-fighting is concentrated on sex, which has now become the "in" sin.

To all of us who are peering into the future, it looks very much as though we're going to lose sex, too—as a sin, that is. We're not going to lose sex. Far from it.

Masters and Johnson have already made it into an exact science. In the biology department at Washington University they're still cutting up pickled lobsters, but over in the annex you know what else they're doing, and by the last edition they'd done it more than five thousand times. Not long ago that would have caused an inquisition.

Dr. Alex Comfort, the British expert on the subject, has written a number of very specific books which make it clear where *he* thinks sex is going in the future. He regards it as "the healthiest and most important human sport" and believes that in the future "we may eventually come to realize that chastity is no more a virtue than malnutrition." He even gives laboratory proof that it's good for you (at least if you're a rat): "It has been shown that in rats regular mating leads to greater longevity and increases resistance to chemical and biological poisons, infections, and stress."[1]

The results aren't in yet for people, but the rats do have one clear advantage over humans: Nobody ever made them feel guilty about it.

One of Comfort's main points about sex is that people who are doing a lot of it are too busy doing it to talk about it, whereas it is "the least sexually active section . . . the 'infra-sex,' who tended to compensate for their animal deficiencies by developing an abnormally strong desire to regulate the conduct of others."[2] I'm not sure where that puts Comfort—or me, either. *We're* both talking about it, aren't we?

Dr. Comfort looks right at sex in the future, and what he sees is group sex, or swinging.[3] He says we practice "serial polygamy" now anyway—or, one spouse at a time—and it's just a step from there to swinging. Why, he says, give yourself completely to any one person? Why fence yourself in? It's difficult to expect any one person to be all things to any other person. Some million-odd swingers go along with that today.

Whether you'll go that far, at least you can see that this point of view is going to strike quite a blow at sex as sin. Sex may get into the same category as shaking hands or playing bingo, and then where will we be?

Sex may even be considered therapeutic in the future, according to a young psychiatrist in Sweden—a country that some people regard as being the closest to the future sexually (and some regard as being closest to perdition). Dr. Lars Ullerstam suggested that sex be used like medicine for mental illness and personal trouble. He thought young men and women should volunteer as "sexual samaritans" to help those people who have a psychological or physical need for sex.[4]

My hunch is that all this will eventually lead, in the future, to what I call the Sexual Bill of Rights.

The Sexual Bill of Rights

Our rights all come slowly, and one after the other. Not too long ago you could be clapped into jail for just standing on a street corner and speaking your mind. You still can, in about half the world. (In the other half, they just don't pay any attention.)

And it's hard to believe that only about a century ago, there wasn't even the right to eat:

"You mean the right to eat—free?"

"At least not to starve, yes."

"*Give* it to 'em, without work? Nobody'd work! Whole world would go to pot!"

Well, it didn't end the world, giving people the right not to be hungry.

In the future we'll have a Sexual Bill of Rights. Everyone will have the right to sexual fulfillment if he or she wants it, even those who are poor, crippled, ugly, a bit too shy, or too old. These people, like the rest of us, often have deep yearnings and a real need for physical love. Today they have no chance to get it; they simply remain deprived and frustrated all their lives. Ullerstam would call these people "the sexual minorities." And they have a right. Any human being has the right.

Which is more immoral: being unselfish with them or just closing the door in their faces, as we do now?

Of course, it could get pretty complicated:

"But, Mrs. Dickson, your card has *already* been punched three times today!"

"Oh, I know, dear boy, but the late Mr. Dickson, bless him, *did* get me *terribly* used to it. Be a love and punch me once again, will you?"

Limits will certainly have to be set.

And we'll have to consider the spouses of some of our "sexual samaritans":

"Johnny, darling, I *know* it's your job, but *do* save a bit for me, won't you?"

"Mustn't be selfish, must we, pet?"

And unfortunately, if it's a government agency, there will inevitably be a lot of printed forms to fill in:

> *Preferences?* (Be specific, please. Block letters!)
>
> *Any little quirks?* (Don't be bashful. How are we to know?)
>
> *Any* big *quirks?* (We *do* have to draw the line somewhere!)
>
> *Just the regular service, or do you need a complete overhaul?*
>
> *Do you have anything you'd like to donate?* (Give all the dreadful details, please.)

And it may do a lot for technological unemployment:

"How does your husband like working for that new government agency?"

"He says he feels more secure. He was replaced in his last three jobs by computers. He says this is something *no* computer can ever do!"

Not *ever?* It's no good being complacent. Today technology stops at nothing.

How to Make a Mistress of Your Computer

Some of our future prophets feel that sex will no longer be considered sinful simply because it will seem so mild and pedestrian in comparison with the new power-pleasures. Just ordinary human, physical sex may seem almost ascetic, like running a mile before breakfast.

Have you heard about those rats?

Some devilish scientists found the pleasure centers in the rats' brains and plugged them into an electrical stimulator. Flip the switch and the rat has instant ecstasy. They let the rat try it, gave him a button to push, and just left it up to him how often he'd push it. Food, drink, and the sexiest lady rat were all there, just awaiting his pleasure. Did he want them? "Don't be old-fashioned!" said the rat, and pushed the button six thousand times an hour. He couldn't be bothered even to rest. And you can imagine how *she* felt. The report didn't say whether they hooked *her* up after he was through.[5]

Dolphins, who have bigger brains than ours, have been hooked up, too. They are simply ecstatic about it. How do you think the navy gets them to do all those things, like diving down five hundred feet to recover stray torpedoes? Those dolphins will do just about anything for an electrical fix.

Will it work for humans? Oh, will it! The pleasure-center experts believe that humans have at least *six* of these ecstasy spots, just waiting for electrification. Once we're all plugged in, having sex may become just a few push-ups in mixed company, like asking a sultan to play post office. Even drugs may become old hat.

"Plug me in, dear, unhook the phone, and plug yourself up, too. We're off!"

Assuming six or more pleasure centers, they could be wired to a keyboard and become like notes on a scale. Perhaps, by variations in intensity or modulation, the ecstasy could be shaped in tone or timbre (we'll obviously need a whole set of new words here). There might be the equivalent of higher and lower octaves, and we could create pleasure music hundreds of times more enjoyable than the music of sound alone. It might very well include the pleasures of sound-music, mixed with excruciating pleasures of sex, and beauty and luscious taste and heavenly scents, and surely other exquisite pleasures beyond our present ability to imagine.

The delights could be played in titillating combinations—perhaps in sequence, like melodies, or in combination, like harmony, and in melodic harmonies, and in counterpoint. Pleasure composers could write ecstatic fugues, Bach to the thousandth power, sonatas, rondos, symphonies, and oratorios of sensation. Lovers could have private melodies to play, not *to* one another, but *upon* one another, finding special, personal preferences. The narcissistic could write little ingrown canticles to play upon themselves, madrigals of cerebral masturbation.

It could be an art of multiple ecstasy, so sensitive and delicate and intoxicatingly enjoyable that every other art would seem pedestrian, a pleasure so sublime it would mock paradise, a vice so infinite it would be worth damnation.

And all this might use less electricity than an electric shaver and be a hundred times less damaging to the biosphere than riding a motorbike around the block.

And it might be the final answer to the population explosion. The ultimate in birth control is something that is more hedonistic than the real thing. The problem might well be in the opposite direction.

Is there a computer that says there can be no more growth in the world? Where then, sir, does this sort of thing fit into your electric philosophy?

And what will happen to sin, if sex becomes nothing more than a duty to humanity? My prediction is that electrical hedonism may develop, sin-wise, in two different ways. The first is that the hard-faced puritans of the world are going to declare that electronic pleasure is a sin of the first magnitude, two points more damnable than incest, if only because it's so much fun. They will do their best to endow it with a crushing sense of guilt.

The other way is that some will declare electric ecstasy to be not only respectable, but somehow exalted, or, as some may say, *saintly*. Have you ever looked into the history of religious ecstasy? The British anthropologist I. M. Lewis has, in a fascinating book called *Ecstatic Religion*. Some of these phenomena are Christian, like the raptures of Saint Teresa with her "spouse," the spirit of Jesus—captured forever in mid-rapture by Bernini, in marble; or, like those of the Tennessee snake handlers, members of the Dolly Pond Baptist Church.

Many are not Christian, like the ecstasies of Haitian women, possessed by the snake god Damballah; or Eskimos, temporarily inhabited by the spirits of the seals they have had to—regrettably—eat. There are many others. All of them seem, in the pictures, to be experiencing the same almost unbearable pleasures, even though the inspiration varies. They are, you might say, having all that fun, and keeping their respectability, too.

There will surely be people who will make a cult out of the electrical wowsers, just as there are people today who believe that eating certain kinds of mushrooms brings them closer to infinite truth, whatever that may be.

To take a really pragmatic view, we may, in the future, have to create sins with real, solid stuffings in them. Sinners will be those who actually *hurt* other people or damage the planet, committing sins like throwing away beer bottles, burning your leaves instead of composting them, not recycling your newspaper, leaving your motor running—or perhaps even having a motor at all—voting against the sewage treatment plant, or even (in violation of the encyclicals of Saint Barry of Commoner) buying a nylon shirt or buying *anything* that won't rot.

All these dastardly acts will, in the future, be much more harmful to the earth and to your fellowman than the old-fashioned sins like sleeping with your neighbor's wife—assuming, of course, that you've taken the proper precautions against exploding the population and that, for the sake of neighborliness, you've let him sleep with yours.

So we may have to work these newly venal sins into something properly leering and lip-smacking. We'll have to supply scarlet letters to be worn on the breast like *H* for Harvard—no longer *A* for adultery, but *B* for beer bottles, *C* for chemical fertilizers, *I*, not for egotism or incest, but for insecticide, and *P* (the most damning), not for Princeton, but for pollution. We might put the sinners into a pillory and pelt them with biodegradable material.

16

HOW DOOMSDAY CAN HELP US ALL

Now, then, do you still believe the world will end to-morrow? I don't. Does that mean that all the doomsday criers were simply lying? Is it all a fake? No, it's not. If we keep on going the way we have been, we *are* doomed, and not in the far distant future, but soon enough to affect our children or their children.

But we'll have the satisfaction of knowing we've done it all ourselves. Nobody did it *to* us.

There are no green-eyed monsters. The sun will keep on shining for millions more years. We are now, as never before, the lords of the earth, and even of all the planets circling the sun. We have thoroughly mastered this world, almost completely whipped all contagion and disease, and every living thing is here at our pleasure. There is no force in the whole solar system that can challenge us in any way, and there's not a breath of any other kind of intelligent life within at least four light-years—and it may be thousands. It may even be—nowhere else.

What are we afraid of? The doomsday fellows are all agreed at least on this: Us. Ourselves. We are completely masters of our fate. Nobody can hurt us but ourselves.

Do we really plan to destroy ourselves and our planet? Do we honestly plan to commit planetary suicide?

I can't believe we're doomed, but I'm glad we thought of the possibility. For the first time in the history of man we have a life-and-death concern for our planet. And for the first time we realize that your fate and mine are tied inextricably to those of all men.

We really knew it before, in an intellectual way, but perhaps we didn't feel it emotionally until we saw the pictures of the little blue planet floating there all alone in space.

The main thing is not to believe the people who say, "Whatever we do, we're doomed." And when they say, "No more growth is possible," then I say, "What kind of growth do you mean?" If they mean bigger cars, two swimming pools for every backyard, and bigger piles of scrapped affluence, then I agree. That kind of bloated, gluttonous growth will have to be abandoned. We'll have to live within our planetary means.

Real growth is in pleasure, knowledge, and skills—growth in the enjoyment of life, not just for the rich peoples of the world, but for all.

There's no limit to growth in these directions. It will take an enormous amount of work and a great deal of tender care.

We shall have to start acting as if this is the only planet we have.

BIBLIOGRAPHICAL NOTES

CHAPTER I

1. Jay W. Forrester, *World Dynamics* (Cambridge, Mass.: Wright-Allen Press, 1971), p. 100, graph.
2. Ibid., p. 105.
3. *Science*, March 10, 1972, p. 1092.
4. Ibid., p. 1088.
5. T. W. Oerlemans, M. M. J. Tellings, and H. De Vries, article in *Nature*, August 4, 1972, pp. 251ff.
6. *24 Heures* (Lausanne), January 29, 1973, p. 43.

CHAPTER 2

1. Quoted in John Maddox, *The Doomsday Syndrome* (New York: McGraw-Hill, 1972).
2. Rachel Carson, *Silent Spring* (Boston: Houghton Mifflin), 1962.
3. Barry Commoner, *The Closing Circle* (New York: Knopf, 1971), p. 80.
4. Ibid., p. 111.
5. Maddox, *Doomsday Syndrome*, p. 20.
6. Ibid., p. 154.
7. Ibid., p 175.
8. Barbara Ward and René Dubos, *Only One Earth: The Care and Maintenance of a Small Planet* (London: Penguin Books, 1972), p. 104.
9. Maddox, *Doomsday Syndrome*, p. 132.

10. Ward and Dubos, *Only One Earth*, p. 27.
11. Ibid., p. 110.
12. Ibid., p. 232.
13. Edwin G. Dolan, *TANSTAAFL: The Economic Strategy for Environmental Crisis* (New York: Holt, Rinehart & Winston, 1971).
14. Ward and Dubos, *Only One Earth*, p. 124.
15. Ibid., p. 126.
16. *National Geographic*, November 1972, p. 673.
17. *Closing Circle*, p. 188.
18. *National Geographic*, November 1972, p. 654.

CHAPTER 3

1. Bernard C. Patten, ed., *Systems Analysis and Simulation in Ecology* (New York: Academic Press, 1971). Reviewed in *Science*, February 25, 1972, p. 742.

CHAPTER 4

1. Richard Neuhaus, *In Defense of People* (New York: Macmillan, 1971), p. 123.
2. Ibid., p. 128.

CHAPTER 5

1. Ward and Dubos, *Only One Earth*, p. 41.
2. Paul Ehrlich, *The Population Bomb* (San Francisco: Sierra Club, 1972). William and Paul Paddock, *Famine—1975!* (Boston: Little, Brown, 1967).
3. *Scientific American*, March 1973, p. 22.
4. *Time*, April 30, 1973, p. 51.
5. *International Herald Tribune*, March 3, 1973.

CHAPTER 6

1. Ward and Dubos, *Only One Earth*, p. 176.
2. Tomas Frejka, *Scientific American*, March 1973.
3. *The New York Times*, June 7, 1972.

CHAPTER 7

1. Donald R. Levi and Dale Colyer, "Legal Remedies for Pollution Abatement," *Science*, March 10, 1972, pp. 1085ff.

CHAPTER 8

1. *Fortune*, April 1972, p. 68.
2. Ward and Dubos, *Only One Earth*, p. 190.
3. Ibid., p. 189.
4. *Fortune*, April 1972, p. 146.
5. Ibid., p. 150.

CHAPTER 10

1. Peter Goldmark, "Communication and the Community," *Scientific American*, September 1972.
2. Ibid., pp. 145–146.
3. Brenda Maddox, *Beyond Babel* (New York: Simon & Schuster, 1972).
4. Ibid., p. 166.
5. Hiroshi Inosi, "Communications Network," *Scientific American*, September 1972, pp. 117–128.
6. Maddox, *Beyond Babel*, p. 100.
7. *The New York Times*, October 3 and 15, 1972.
8. Ibid., June 17, 1972.

CHAPTER 11

1. Maddox, *Beyond Babel*, p. 121.

CHAPTER 12

1. Alvin Toffler, *Future Shock* (London: Bodley Head, 1970), p. 141.
2. Maddox, *Beyond Babel*, p. 131.
3. Ibid., p. 132.

4. Ibid.
5. Ibid., p. 133.
6. Ibid., p. 135.

CHAPTER 13

1. Arne Tiselius and Sam Nilsson, eds., *The Place of Value in a World of Facts*, proceedings of the Fourteenth Nobel Symposium (Stockholm: Almqvist and Wiksell, 1970).
2. G. Rattray Taylor, *The Biological Time Bomb* (London: Panther, 1969), pp. 154–155.
3. Ibid., p. 155.
4. Joshua Lederberg in Tiselius and Nilsson, *Place of Value*, p. 49.
5. Taylor, *Biological Time Bomb*, p. 182.
6. Tiselius and Nilsson, *Place of Value*, p. 52.
7. Taylor, *Biological Time Bomb*, p. 31.
8. Ibid., p. 32.
9. Ibid., p. 183.
10. Ibid., p. 184.
11. "The Urge to Self-Destruction," Tiselius and Nilsson, *Place of Value*, p. 300.

CHAPTER 14

1. B. F. Skinner, *Beyond Freedom and Dignity* (New York: Knopf, 1971).
2. Many of the pigeon-facts about Dr. Skinner came from an excellent *Time* cover story: September 20, 1971.

CHAPTER 15

1. Alex Comfort, *Sex in Society* (London: Penguin, 1964), pp. 26, 45, 97.
2. Ibid., p. 46.
3. *Time*, January 8, 1973.
4. *Observer* (London), September 6, 1964.
5. Herman Kahn and B. Bruce-Briggs, *Things to Come* (New York: Macmillan, 1972).

INDEX

Index

Index

Index

Wankel engine, 83
Ward, Barbara, 29–30, 31, 32, 34–35, 63–64, 91, 94
Washington University, 204
Water Pollution Control Act, 71
Webster, N.Y., 97
Weed killers, 22–23
Westinghouse Corporation, 89, 90–91, 94–95, 98
Wildlife, 46–50
Wildlife Fund, 48

World Dynamics (Forrester), 4–19
World population, 52

Xerox Corporation, 97
XP (experience), 122–123
X-ray crystallography, 142

Zamenhof, F., 163
Zero population growth, 60